COURAGEOUS CRIMEFIGHTERS

COURAGEOUS CRIMEFIGHTERS

Robert Italia

The Oliver Press, Inc.
Minneapolis

Library of Congress Cataloging-in-Publication Data

Italia, Bob, 1955-
Courageous crimefighters / Robert Italia.
p.   cm. — (Profiles)
Includes bibliographical references and index.
ISBN 1-881508-21-8
1. Detectives—Biography—Juvenile literature. 2. Criminal investigation—Juvenile literature. 3. Crime prevention—Juvenile literature. I. Title. II. Title: Courageous crimefighters. III. Series: Profiles (Minneapolis, Minn.)
HV7911.A1I73 1995
363.2'092—dc20
[B]
                                            94-22098
                                               CIP
                                                AC

ISBN: 1-881508-21-8
Profiles XVI
Printed in the United States of America

99 98 97 96 95   8 7 6 5 4 3 2 1

Contents

Their uniforms have changed over time, but today's police still encounter many of the same challenges faced by these nineteenth-century officers.

Introduction

*J*esse James! John Dillinger! Al Capone! Most people are familiar with the names and careers of these infamous men, who gained national attention by breaking the law. But who put an end to their criminal careers? Who were the crimefighters who continually risked their lives to stop these and other notorious foes?

During the nineteenth century, Allan Pinkerton— the first private detective in the United States—established standards for crimefighters that are still in practice today. Samuel Steele, one of the original Mounties, brought law and order to Canada's vast frontier during the late 1800s and became a national hero because of his bravery. Captain Leander H. McNelly of the Texas Rangers, a sickly man who sometimes directed his men from a wagon bed, helped to tame the Old West and

7

became one of the most fabled and fearless Texas Rangers of all time.

Melvin Purvis, the top FBI agent during the 1930s, was responsible for ending the careers of John Dillinger and other well-known gangsters. But Purvis often crossed the line between right and wrong and frequently argued with his superior, J. Edgar Hoover. Thanks to a successful film and television series based loosely on the government's attempts to stop the criminal empire of Al Capone, FBI agent Eliot Ness is one of the most recognizable crimefighters in recent history. Fearless, intelligent, and relentless in his pursuit of the criminal element, Ness fits the perception most people have of a crimefighter.

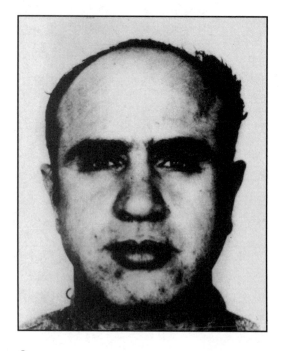

An FBI mug shot of crime lord Al Capone, Eliot Ness's arch enemy during Prohibition

But not all of the crimefighters profiled in this book are known for their gun battles with hardened criminals. Before becoming prime minister of Great Britain, Sir Robert Peel fought crime in the nineteenth century by establishing Scotland Yard, one of the most famous police organizations in the world. During the 1950s and 1960s, Tennessee senator Estes Kefauver also used the power of his political office to battle corruption in business and government. Simon Wiesenthal, another unlikely crimefighter, narrowly escaped death during the Holocaust and devoted his life after World War II to tracking down the Nazis responsible for killing millions of Jews.

At first glance, these courageous crimefighters seem to have little in common. Some were studious and methodical, while others were arrogant and flamboyant. Likewise, the types of crimes these men investigated and the law-enforcement techniques they used depended on the times in which they lived and the dangers they faced. Although they led very different lives, these crimefighters shared a belief in the rights of law-abiding citizens.

Concerned by rising crime statistics in Britain's capital city, Sir Robert Peel (1788-1850) established one of the world's best-known detective agencies in London.

1

Sir Robert Peel
The Legend of Scotland Yard

Sir Robert Peel was not a famous crimefighter. But his keen foresight and deep concern for the welfare of his country led to the establishment of one of the most famous crime fighting organizations in the world—Scotland Yard.

Born on February 5, 1788, Robert Peel was the son of a wealthy, British cotton manufacturer. Using his father's financial influence, Peel entered politics in 1809 when he gained a seat in the British parliament. Peel's interest in law enforcement began while serving as chief secretary of Ireland from 1812 to 1818, where he established an Irish police force. In 1819, Peel became chairman of the British parliamentary currency committee. Peel's rise in politics continued when he accepted the post of Britain's secretary of state for the home department in 1822, where he served until 1830.

Rising crime statistics convinced Peel that improved methods of crime prevention should accompany legal reform. Beginning in 1823, he initiated reform measures in the British prison system and proposed many anti-crime laws. In 1829, he spearheaded the Metropolitan Police Act, which established London's first major police force—the London Metropolitan Police. (Until then, London had been protected by the Bow Street Police, a small band of officers first created in the mid-1700s.)

This new Metropolitan Police force had 1,000 officers its first year and reported to the British parliament through Robert Peel. Because of Peel's efforts, the London police became known as "Peelers," "Bobby's boys," and later as "bobbies." The original headquarters of the force was at 4 Whitehall Place, a part of the Scotland Yard complex. (The building stood on the site of a medieval palace that had housed Scottish royalty when they visited London.)

At first, the new police force encountered little cooperation from the public. Many people thought the Metropolitan Police would oppress common citizens and infringe upon their personal rights. When Scotland Yard

Sir Robert Peel wanted the streets of London to be safe from crime—but many London residents wanted their streets safe from the police.

stationed its first plainclothes police agents on duty in 1842, a public outcry arose against these "spies."

Gradually, however, the British public began to accept—and even respect—the Metropolitan Police. During the 1830s and 1840s, Sir Robert Peel served as Great Britain's prime minister twice and no longer had any direct contact with the police force he had created. By the time Peel died on July 2, 1850, the Metropolitan Police force—popularly called Scotland Yard—was on its way to becoming a legend in fighting crime.

Throughout its history, Scotland Yard has had many famous detectives, including Adolphus Williamson, who

Although British prime minister Robert Peel never worked as a police officer, the detectives of Scotland Yard are still called "bobbies" in his honor.

joined the force during the mid-nineteenth century. After passing a civil service exam, Adolphus—or "Dolly," as his friends called him—was hired by the British War Office. Although he had a promising career in government, he soon told his friends in the War Office that he planned to quit his job.

"Where can you go and do better?" they asked.

"Scotland Yard," he said.

Soon after he was hired as a *constable* (a uniformed officer) for the Metropolitan Police, Adolphus Williamson recovered the Countess of Dudley's stolen jewels. After reading Williamson's clear and detailed police report, the commissioner of Scotland Yard took Williamson out of uniform and added him to the detective force that had become known as "the Yard."

Williamson rapidly climbed to fame. First as a superintendent and then the chief of the Criminal Investigation Department (CID), he became personally known to half the aristocracy in London and to the

A Metropolitan Police officer stands guard outside the entrance to Scotland Yard during the mid-1800s.

majority of the capital's most dangerous criminals. The CID, which was created in 1878, was a small force of detectives who gathered information on criminal activities. (In addition to the CID, the Metropolitan Police also gained a traffic department and the Special Branch investigative unit.)

As Williamson rose through the ranks of the police force, he became friends of the Prince of Wales and William Pinkerton, a member of the famous Pinkerton's National Detective Agency in the United States. Pinkerton said he considered Williamson the greatest detective of all time, and Scotland Yard began to win international respect.

Soon after its creation, Scotland Yard won the respect of William Pinkerton and other top detectives in the United States.

In perhaps his most famous case, Williamson tried to track down the clever thieves who had lifted gold bullion from a British mail train. For 18 months, Williamson searched his files on the criminal underworld, investigated the bullion markets, and listened to thousands of rumors. Despite his hard work, he drew a blank. Then one day, Williamson was visited by a mysterious railroad attendant named Fanny Kay, who said she was in love with a man named Edward "Ted" Agar. "I'd have been Mrs. Edward Agar by now if it hadn't been for those crooks!" she confided.

"Why didn't this Mr. Agar marry you?" he asked.

"Because he knew he might be arrested, and he didn't want me to feel ashamed of being married to a convict," Fanny Kay replied.

"He told you that?"

The woman nodded. "What's more, I believe him. Ted's like that. But that William Pierce is a cold fish." Fanny Kay continued to tell Williamson about how a man named William Pierce met with Ted Agar at various locations in London. "I don't know what it was all about," she said, "because Ted wouldn't tell me about his business activities. But there were this other pair, known as Tester and Burgess."

These names were all new to Williamson. "Where is Pierce now?" he asked.

"I don't know. He's moved, and he's gone with my money." Then, Fanny Kay described the night she had

17

surprised Agar and his friends working over a small furnace. "There was a strong smell. It made me feel sick. I asked Ted what they were doing, and he said they'd been making leather aprons."

Williamson checked dates, asked questions about the smell and the furnace, and came to the incredible conclusion that Agar had been smelting gold bullion! Williamson was sure he was on the right track when he asked Fanny Kay how much money William Pierce was withholding from her.

She said that Pierce still owed her 7,000 British pounds, which was worth about $32,000 in the United States.

Williamson asked the woman why she decided to report this crime. Fanny Kay looked at Williamson and responded, "I'm not letting Pierce get away with cheating me." Apparently Kay was so intent on getting back at Pierce that she had not realized her statements also implicated Agar, whom she wanted to marry.

While detectives searched for William Pierce, Adolphus Williamson paid a visit to the house Fanny Kay had described. He came away more convinced than ever that the gold had been melted down in a small furnace he found there. Williamson deduced that Pierce and Agar were the gold bullion thieves.

Williamson next went to the London Bridge railway station and spoke to the secretary of the London and Southeastern Railway Company. Within a few minutes, he had the addresses of two of the company's employees: Burgess, who worked as a guard, and Tester, who worked as a clerk for the railroad's traffic superintendent. Instead of arresting the two men immediately, Williamson had them followed. Before long, detectives were outside the luxurious home that belonged to a man named William Pierce.

Williamson then visited Agar, who by now was in prison for the theft but hadn't disclosed the names of any of his accomplices. To get Agar to talk, Williamson told him that Pierce had left Fanny Kay very little money to live on. Agar grew furious after hearing this news, then made a full confession of everyone's role in the bullion theft.

Within hours, Williamson's officers arrested Pierce, who had concealed most of the melted gold in a hole in the pantry of his house. In other rooms of the house, the detectives uncovered stocks and bonds, deeds of property, and certificates worth several thousands of British pounds.

The three men Williamson arrested had enough money to hire one of Britain's leading attorneys to defend them at their trial. But fine speeches could not save the wrongdoers from prison. Williamson worked for Scotland Yard for 40 years, and he died shortly after his retirement.

With his strong leadership ability and sharp detective skills, Williamson probably shaped the image of the

19

Yard more than anyone else since Robert Peel founded the organization.

In 1890, the Metropolitan Police entered a new era when their headquarters moved to a new location on the Thames Embankment, alongside London's famous river. The new building was appropriately called New Scotland Yard. By this time, mystery readers had become more familiar with Scotland Yard through the exploits of Sherlock Holmes. Sir Arthur Conan Doyle's fictional detective, who often worked with Scotland Yard in the stories, won tremendous international popularity.

During this period, *real* crime fighting in Scotland Yard was becoming more precise. Sir Edward Henry,

"A Study in Scarlet," the first story featuring detective Sherlock Holmes (right), was published in 1887. Sir Arthur Conan Doyle wrote a total of 38 Holmes mysteries.

another man who added to the prestige of the organization, helped turn crime fighting into a science. In 1900, he published a report that explained how fingerprints could be used as a form of identification. In his report, Henry expanded on the fingerprint classification system that British scientist Francis Galton developed during the late nineteenth century.

As Scotland Yard's new commissioner, Henry demonstrated the practical value of this new means of identification. He claimed that the Galton system surpassed the identification system first introduced by French criminologist Alphonse Bertillon. (Bertillon's system, which French law-enforcement agents began using in 1888, classified people by their body measurements, along with hair and skin coloring.)

The opportunity to prove Henry's theory arrived in what came to be known as the case of the Fox twins. Ebenezer Albert Fox and Albert Ebenezer Fox were experienced poachers who hunted game from protected areas. But the twins were so similar that their Bertillon measurements—including the size of their ears, the width of their heads, and the length their arms, legs and fingers—could not distinguish one from the other. When the police arrested the brothers, they could not be certain which one was Albert and which one was Ebenezer.

The detectives' attempts to tell the Fox brothers apart ended abruptly when Henry, Scotland Yard's leading criminologist, took the fingerprints of each of the twins.

During the late 1800s, French criminologist Alphonse Bertillon (1853-1914) developed a system that used skeletal measurements and other traits to classify criminals. Today, that system has been largely replaced by fingerprinting.

The looping patterns on their fingers were so dissimilar that identification was relatively easy. Clearly, fingerprints could help to confirm someone's identity and help solve criminal cases.

Lawyers and judges, however, remained hard to convince. Time after time, Scotland Yard detectives sought to introduce fingerprint evidence at trials. But judges would declare the fingerprints inadmissible, largely because the British courts had no accepted precedent for admitting this type of evidence. The Yard detectives continued to take suspects' Bertillon measurements as well as their fingerprints, even though the courts accepted only the Bertillon measurements as evidence.

During this time, Sir Edward devised a mathematical formula for classifying and recording fingerprints. Each set of fingerprints was filed under a number ranging from 1 to 32; fingerprints with similar patterns were filed under the same number. But when the detectives compared individual fingerprints within the same number, the police found that each set of fingerprints was different.

By 1902, Sir Edward Henry had recorded more than 1,700 sets of prints. Although the fingerprints proved to be a great help to detectives of the Yard's Criminal Investigation Department, another three years would pass before fingerprints became acceptable evidence in British courts.

The Yard officer who made fingerprint history was Chief Inspector Frederick Fox. In 1905, local police summoned Fox to the London's Deptford district, where a shopkeeper and his wife had died from severe blows to the head. When Fred Fox arrived in Deptford, the police took him to the building where the deaths had occurred. In an upstairs bedroom, Fox discovered overturned furniture, drawers and cupboards that had been emptied onto the floor, and an empty cash box that lay on its side. Under the bed, Fox found the tray that belonged inside the metal cash box, and there was a thumb print on the tray.

Using a clean cloth, Fox carefully wrapped the cash box and the tray in paper, then carted them away to the fingerprint department at Scotland Yard. The inspector who conducted the fingerprint tests established that neither the shopkeeper nor his wife had made the thumb print on the tray.

Fred Fox's task was to find a person who had made that print. Fox concluded that, after entering the building, the burglar ran into the shopkeeper, who had been awakened by the intruder. Not finding much money in the shop or in the cash box, the culprit—or culprits—turned brutal and beat both the shopkeeper and his wife to death.

After further investigation, Fox discovered that there were witnesses to the crime. A milkman had noticed two young men run off after leaving the shop on High Street. A girl who was heading down the street at the time had also seen these same, poorly dressed men scurry away after leaving the shop.

These descriptions did not prove very helpful, however. For one week, two Scotland Yard inspector-detectives checked all known criminal cases in the Deptford district. This was a huge task because the area was frequented by hoodlums. But then one detective reported that he had not located two of the suspects he had been trying to check on.

Next, some of the people living in Deptford told Fox about a young woman called Annie who had been seen in the company of the two men, who were brothers. But she, too, had been missing for a few days. Following up a lead, Fox found Annie, who was recovering from a disfiguring black eye. The inspector-detective learned that Alf Stratton, the elder of the brothers, had punched Annie in the face.

When the police found Alf at a pub, they arrested him. Shortly thereafter, they arrested his brother, Albert, who was staying in a cheap hotel. The police held the Stratton brothers in custody for one week. During that time, the officers at the Yard completed their fingerprint tests and found that the mark on the cash box tray matched Alf Stratton's right thumb print.

During the trial, one of the Scotland Yard detective-inspectors involved in the case used a large chart and some impressions taken from the fingers of a jury member to show the accuracy of fingerprints as a form of identification. The judge hearing the case admitted fingerprints as evidence for the jury to consider, but he cautioned the jury not to rely too heavily on this new kind of evidence. After two hours of debating all of the evidence, the jury returned with a guilty verdict, and the judge sentenced the Stratton brothers to death. They were hanged weeks later, largely because of a thumb print left at the scene of the crime.

In 1967, Scotland Yard again moved, this time to the Westminster area near Britain's Houses of Parliament. Today, fingerprints are used routinely in police work across the globe, and the legend of Scotland Yard has continued.

Although Allan Pinkerton (1819-1884) became the first private detective in the United States almost by chance, the national detective agency he founded has survived for nearly 150 years.

2

Allan Pinkerton
The Original Private Eye

*A*llan Pinkerton did not set out to be a crimefighter. To avoid political persecution, Pinkerton fled his native Scotland in 1842. In the United States, he became a crimefighter almost accidentally, and soon afterward created the first national detective agency. During his 28-year career, Pinkerton investigated more than 1,000 crimes, and his slogan, "We Never Sleep," inspired the term "private eye."

Allan Pinkerton was born on August 25, 1819, in Glasgow, Scotland. At age ten, Pinkerton got his first job, running errands for a pattern maker. About two years later, a cooper named William McCauley hired Allan as his apprentice. For seven years, Allan learned to make barrels and casks, and he eventually became a master craftsman. As a teenager, he joined the Chartist political movement. The Chartists wanted to make several reforms, such as giving all adult males—not just property owners—the right to vote.

Allan worked at his trade by day and met with the Chartists at night. He also fell in love with a young woman named Joan Carfrae, who also sympathized with the Chartist movement. Before they could set a wedding date, however, Allan learned that the authorities were planning to arrest him as an enemy of the government. In 1842, he and Joan decided to leave Scotland in haste. They soon married and boarded a ship headed for Canada.

After a few months, the Pinkertons bought a horse and wagon and traveled westward to Chicago. There, Allan Pinkerton finally found work as a cooper, making barrels at a brewery, and in 1843 opened his own shop in the nearby town of Dundee. He and Joan now lived in a comfortable house in a pleasant community. They also had a young son named William.

One day, when Pinkerton rowed out to a small island in nearby Fox River to cut some wood, he noticed a site where a group of people had camped but had tried to cover up signs of their presence. Charred campfire embers were scattered about, and Pinkerton spotted half of a burned five-dollar bill.

This puzzled Pinkerton because he did not believe that people from Dundee would have hidden traces of their campsite. Counterfeiters had plagued the county for years, so Pinkerton suspected the charred bill was counterfeit. Why else would someone burn it?

Pinkerton told his story to the local sheriff and suggested watching the island. One night shortly thereafter, a deputy saw a campfire and rowed back to Dundee with the news. The sheriff sent a posse to the island, and the men returned with a printing press, and special inks used in counterfeiting, as well as a small band of counterfeiters.

Allan Pinkerton became a local hero overnight, and his neighbors declared that the young cooper had made Dundee free of counterfeiters. One local newspaper wrote, "As a detective, Mr. Pinkerton has no superior, and we doubt if he has an equal in the country." Within a few months, Pinkerton's barrel-making business increased, and he expanded his shop and hired several assistants. In 1846, Allan became deputy sheriff for his community.

Six months later, Sheriff William Church of nearby Cook County asked Pinkerton to move to Chicago and become a special agent. Pinkerton would have no special title, but he would be doing various kinds of police work.

After discussing the proposition with his wife, Pinkerton left one of his assistants in charge of his

After helping to stop a band of counterfeiters in Dundee, Illinois, Allan Pinkerton gave up his career as a cooper to investigate crimes.

business, and the Pinkerton family moved to Chicago. There, Allan Pinkerton investigated murders, burglaries, and assaults. He was also busy investigating fraud, extortion, and blackmail cases for the Chicago post office—and soon discovered the postmaster's nephew had stolen $1,500.

When Chicago wanted to create a police department, Special Agent Pinkerton wrote 50 pages of suggestions and recommendations for the new organization. As a result, he was named the first detective on the Chicago force. Detective Pinkerton went to work early and came home late, and his name began appearing in the newspapers often as an arresting officer.

In 1850, after Pinkerton solved a series of thefts for a major railroad, three railroad presidents suggested that he go into business for himself. They offered him $10,000 a year to protect their property, and he could afford to hire enough employees to pursue other kinds of detective work as well.

After careful consideration, Pinkerton accepted the offer and named his business Pinkerton's National Detective Agency. Its trademark would be a wide-open eye. Joan Pinkerton came up with the company slogan, "We Never Sleep." Allan Pinkerton hired a small group of trustworthy men who wanted to be detectives, and he developed "ten principles" for the company, which said, in part, that Pinkerton agents could not gamble, drink

ESTABLISHED IN 1850

The Pinkerton agency's office logo inspired the term "private eye" for private detective.

liquor, smoke tobacco, or publish details of their experiences in newspaper or magazine articles.

After learning about these ten principles, many Chicago police officers declared that Pinkerton's agency would not last six months. Ironically, Pinkerton did so well solving his first railroad cases that business fell off due to a lack of further crime. However, after Joan Pinkerton suggested that the company expand by soliciting nonrailroad clients, new work poured in.

Abraham Lincoln's election to the presidency in November 1860 pleased Allan Pinkerton greatly because he admired Lincoln's reservations about slavery, a growing issue between northern and southern states, where much of the economy depended on slave labor.

Allan Pinkerton, who strongly opposed slavery, had used his cooper business as a secret hideout for southern slaves escaping to northern states or Canada.

But hostility toward Lincoln ran high in the southern states, and there were rumors that an anti-Lincoln colonel living in Baltimore was openly calling for an insurrection late in February 1861, when Lincoln was due to pass through there on his way to Washington, D.C., for the presidential inauguration. This uprising could harm both the railroads and the new president.

When the railroad officials asked Pinkerton to investigate, he rented an office in Baltimore and began receiving reports from his agents, whom he had stationed at various points along the Philadelphia railroad right-of-way between Baltimore and the Susquehanna Ferry.

Early one morning, Pinkerton received dreadful news. Plans for the Baltimore uprising now included a conspiracy to seize the city of Washington once Lincoln was killed. Pinkerton and his men had to act quickly. When Lincoln arrived in Philadelphia on February 22, Pinkerton warned him of the planned assassination in Baltimore and proposed to take the president-elect directly to Washington that night. But this would require cancelling his speeches in Philadelphia and Harrisburg, which Lincoln refused to do.

After raising the flag over Independence Hall in Philadelphia, the president-elect rode in a carriage to the special train that would take him to Harrisburg, the capital of Pennsylvania. Five minutes before the train was due to leave, one of Lincoln's aides delivered an urgent dispatch from Washington. The message warned the president-elect about an assassination plot against him in Baltimore. Lincoln was now ready to proceed with Pinkerton's plans.

The train left the station for the state capital with two Pinkerton operatives aboard, thoroughly briefed and heavily armed. Pinkerton arranged with the American Telegraph Company to have the Philadelphia office intercept all messages that came over their wires from Harrisburg.

The presidential banquet in Harrisburg started at 5 P.M. One hour after the dinner began, Lincoln slipped away from the table with the excuse that he was suffering from a slight headache. But instead of returning to his upstairs room, he met the Pinkerton agents at a side entrance of the hotel, where a carriage waited for him.

With its shades pulled down, the carriage avoided the crowds at the front of the hotel and headed for a railroad crossing at the outskirts of Harrisburg. There, Lincoln boarded the train, accompanied by two Pinkerton agents and three members of Lincoln's party.

The train carrying Lincoln sped eastward to the station in Philadelphia. There, the president-elect and the agents transferred to a carriage that took them, by a roundabout route, to the Philadelphia railroad station on Carpenter Street. They waited in the shadow of a high fence while Allan Pinkerton took a quick look around. Then, he led them through the yards to the Washington train.

The Washington-bound train left the station around midnight. The train stopped in Baltimore and, after a short delay, resumed its course for the nation's capital. Allan Pinkerton could relax now. The president-elect was safe.

Two months later, the president would need more protection. On April 12, 1861, Fort Sumter—a federal military post off the coast of Charleston in South Carolina—was attacked by forces from the southern states. This attack would lead the United States into the Civil War.

That day, Pinkerton received a wire that read: "Have heard of your achievement in protecting the president and would appreciate your coming to see me in Columbus. Observe caution. If you telegraph me, be sure to use only your first name. Let no one know your plans." The telegraph was signed by Major General George McClellan, commander of the Ohio Volunteers.

In Columbus, Pinkerton met with McClellan, who had fought with distinction during the Mexican War. McClellan asked Pinkerton to oversee a soon-to-be-established division of Union soldiers from Ohio, Illinois, and Indiana. Anxious to play a part in the war effort, Pinkerton accepted this important job and received the rank of major. He knew one of his trusted assistants could take over the detective agency in Chicago.

In late July 1861, George McClellan and Allan Pinkerton attended a conference with President Lincoln

Four years after Allan Pinkerton (left) saved his life, President Abraham Lincoln (1809-1865) was assassinated by actor John Wilkes Booth in the Ford's Theater in Washington, D.C.

to establish the first secret service in the United States. Lincoln felt the Union needed a "secret service unit" because southern spies were invading the North, and the president wanted Pinkerton to head this new organization in Washington. The Union needed to put hundreds of operatives into the field to learn the South's military plans. (The official U.S. Secret Service was established by the Department of Treasury in 1865, the year the Civil War ended.)

During the war, Pinkerton's detective office back in Chicago kept Pinkerton informed of the agency's affairs. In March 1863, Nathan Moroney, a bank manager, stole $40,000 from the Adams Express Company. Pinkerton took a leave of absence from his government duties and directed the investigation into this robbery. Within a month, Pinkerton and his men rounded up the criminals and returned $39,600 to Adams Express. (Moroney had already spent $400.)

Nothing contributed more to the success of the agency's work in the Adams Express case than Pinkerton's national criminal file. This file, which he had started before the war, bulged with facts on thousands of known criminals. It included photographs and biographical information, noting each subject's physical characteristics, special methods of operation, and likely companions and hideouts. Until law enforcement agencies adopted the Bertillon classification system during the 1880s, police from across the United States were constantly in touch with Pinkerton's agency because they needed the invaluable information contained in its files.

During the mid-1870s, the Pinkerton agency tackled one of its toughest assignments—the capture of the James Gang. Jesse and Frank James, working with criminals such as the Younger brothers—Cole, Jim, Bob, and John—had begun to rob banks in the Midwest. At that time, many people thought banks, which charged high interest rates on loans, seemed cruel and unsympathetic to ordinary citizens. Thus, some people regarded bank robbers as heroes fighting injustice.

In 1873, when the James Gang started robbing trains as well as banks, the public grew weary and frightened of the the outlaws' crime spree. A group of governors in the Midwest hired the Pinkerton's National Detective Agency to capture the James brothers and bring them to justice.

One Pinkerton agent volunteered to act as an intelligence agent in the areas frequented by the gang. He was hired as a farm hand and soon became acquainted with Frank and Jesse James. In January 1875, he wired Pinkerton that the James brothers would be visiting their relatives in Kansas in about two weeks. Pinkerton agents immediately left for Kansas City and set up secret headquarters at a hotel there.

On January 5, 1875, Pinkerton received a message that Frank and Jesse James had been seen at the farm of Reuben "Doc" Samuels, Jesse's stepfather. At midnight,

Jesse James (1847-1882), who served as a Confederate scout during the Civil War, took up a career of crime after the war ended in 1865.

the posse—led by William Pinkerton, Allan's eldest son—surrounded the dark homestead where Samuels lived. The Pinkerton agents broke one of the windows of the house and threw in balls of cotton that had been soaked in kerosene, which set the Samuels' house on fire. One of the agents then threw in a hand grenade that had been wadded up in cotton. Thinking the grenade was another fire ball that hadn't been lit, Samuels threw the grenade into the fireplace, where it exploded.

Reuben Samuels was only slightly injured. But Jesse's mother, Zerelda, lost an arm in the explosion, and Jesse's younger half-brother, Archie Samuels, died from his injuries several days later. After the explosion, regional newspapers denounced Allan and William Pinkerton for a "dastardly deed, conceived in cowardice and executed in gore," and rumors spread that Jesse James intended to kill William Pinkerton.

Three months later, Pinkerton thought the time was right to send another posse into Missouri to apprehend the James brothers. Meanwhile, the gang stole approximately $40,000 in gold and cash by robbing trains. After dividing the loot, Jesse and Frank headed back to Clay County, Missouri, and the Younger brothers rode on to Texas. Soon afterward, William Pinkerton organized an improved intelligence system in Clay County.

In September 1876, eight members of the James Gang thundered into Northfield, Minnesota, raiding the First National Bank and killing cashier J. L. Haywood. Local citizens fought back, however, and killed two of the bandits. The survivors, with Jesse in the lead, galloped out of Northfield. After five days of wandering through the countryside, Jesse and Frank James split off from the rest of their band and headed for Shieldville, Minnesota.

By this time, local sheriffs, Pinkerton agents, and vigilantes had combined forces to form a huge army. Although the James brothers were not captured, the band led by Cole Younger was less fortunate. In a gun battle outside the town of Madelia in southern Minnesota, the posse wounded three of the Younger brothers and killed other members of the gang.

The posse took their prisoners to the Flanders Hotel, which also served as jail and hospital for the town. There, Allan Pinkerton interviewed Cole Younger, who readily admitted his identity to Pinkerton. But he refused to admit that Frank and Jesse James had taken part in the attempted Northfield robbery. The Younger brothers stood trial when they were well enough to appear before

Cole Younger, who was captured following the bank raid in Northfield, Minnesota, wrote this obscure note to tell authorities he refused to squeal on the other members of the James Gang.

a court. The judge sentenced each to life at the state prison in Stillwater.

For about three years, there was no news from Clay County, Missouri, as Jesse James had gone into hiding and was living with relatives out of state under an assumed name. Many people assumed the outlaw must have died. Then rumors reached Kansas City, Missouri, that Jesse James was back in the state and had formed a new gang.

In October 1879, five masked bandits flagged a train near Glendale, Missouri, and leaped aboard. The robbers made off with more than $35,000. William Pinkerton followed the outlaws' trail. He covered hundreds of miles on horseback to find information about the James Gang, but most witnesses were unwilling to give information. Eventually, however, he learned the identity of the new gang members.

In March 1881, Frank and Jesse James led their gang in the robbery of a stagecoach near Muscle Shoals, Alabama. In July, they robbed $6,000 from a bank in Riverton, Iowa. William Pinkerton arrived in Iowa two days later, but the James brothers had too far of a head start for him to find them.

William and Allan Pinkerton began to apply more pressure. Operatives covered areas in four states, watching Jesse James's friends and the brothers' farmhouse in Kearny, Missouri. The agents investigated houses in remote places that might offer the outlaws shelter. Other Pinkerton agents traveled in the trains and express cars that the outlaws might try to board and rob. Governor Thomas Crittenden of Missouri offered a reward of $10,000 for the capture and conviction of either Frank or Jesse James, and Missouri railroads—afraid of being robbed by the gang—supplied the funds.

The Pinkertons' continual pursuit caused several criminals to leave the James Gang. But the notorious career of Jesse James did not end at the hands of William Pinkerton or one of the other detectives. In the spring of 1882, one of Jesse James's cousins—19-year-old Bob Ford—met with Governor Crittenden to talk over the reward for the outlaw. On the morning of April 3,

Governor Thomas Crittenden (1832-1909), who held office from 1881 to 1885, earned a reputation for ending criminal activity in Missouri.

Ford shot and killed Jesse in his own home while the outlaw was straightening a picture on the wall.

On October 5, Frank James gave himself up to Governor Crittenden in Jefferson City, Missouri. The state tried him for the murder of a stonemason during a holdup in 1881, but the jury found him not guilty and Frank James quickly slipped into obscurity.

The pursuit of the James Gang proved to be Allan Pinkerton's last case, for he retired later that year at the age of 63. His two sons, William and Robert, took over management of the agency while their father began a

Although he had been an accomplice to his outlaw brother Jesse for several years, Frank James (1843-1915) was never convicted of a crime.

book on his adventures as a detective. In the summer of 1884, while working on the galley proofs of *Thirty Years a Detective*, Pinkerton suffered a massive stroke. He died, without recovering consciousness, on July 1. Joan, his wife, died two years later.

William and Robert Pinkerton were good detectives and administrators and opened new branches of the Pinkerton agency in Boston, Denver, St. Paul, and Kansas City. Today, Pinkerton's National Detective Agency is recognized as the world's largest private agency. With offices in almost every U.S. state and in Canada, the organization has grown into a corporation of more than 13,000 employees.

Early in his career, Allan Pinkerton wrote, "The criminal must pay his debt to society, but must not be hunted and persecuted after he has done so. Justice and human decency demand that we help him to become an honest and reputable citizen." Those principles guided his life as a crimefighter and the future of his agency.

*Samuel Steele (1851–1919), one of Canada's
most celebrated Mounties, dedicated his life to
protecting his country's western frontier.*

3

Samuel Steele
Canada's Greatest Mounty

*W*hen Samuel Steele joined the Northwest Mounted Police at its founding in 1873, his physical strength, skill as a horseback rider, and fierce determination made him an ideal recruit for the new force. Over the years, Steele brought order to the growing population on Canada's western frontier.

Samuel Steele's father, Elmes Steele, was a captain in Britain's Royal Navy. He was 51 when he emigrated to Canada from Great Britain. His wife died in 1846, and two years later he married a woman named Anne

Macdonald. Their son, Samuel Benfield Steele, was born in the town of Purbrook (in present-day Ontario) on January 5, 1851. The Steeles eventually moved to Orillia, where Sam soon rose to the top of his class at the private school in town.

Sam's mother died when he was 9 years old, and his father died five years later. The loss of both his parents forced Sam to care for himself at an early age. Soon after his 14th birthday, he took intensive officer courses in Toronto by convincing the army recruiters he was 16. In 1867, he found employment as a store clerk in the village of Clarksburg, near Orillia. Despite his young age, the leading citizens of Clarksburg wanted to place Sam Steele in command of the local militia company.

Why did they ask a 16 year old to command the militia? Because no one in Clarksburg was better qualified. Sam Steele was a skilled marksman, and he had topped his class in his army officer's courses. Feeling he was too young to head the local militia company, Steele instead joined the First Ontario Rifles and went to Fort Henry in Kingston. There, he was a member of the artillery school in the first Canadian Permanent Force, which had been created to replace the departing British regular troops, who had protected the area. Steele was the 23rd man to join the modern Canadian army, and he was soon promoted to the rank of sergeant, the first of many promotions he would earn.

In the spring of 1873, the Canadian government established a regular armed presence in western Canada. Major James Morrow Walsh came to Ottawa to recruit men for a force that would be known as the Northwest Mounted Police. Steele, who was in Ottawa on a brief tour of duty with his battery, rushed to see Major Walsh and join the new organization.

The Northwest Mounted Police Act received government approval on May 23, 1873. (Originally, the organization was going to be called the Northwest Mounted Rifles, but the name had worried Canada's neighbors in the United States.) The Canadian legislation called for no more than 300 healthy men of good character between the ages of 18 and 40, who were able to ride and to read and write English or French.

Without uniforms or equipment, the first recruits assembled at Prescott Junction on October 2, 1873. Then they traveled to Prince Arthur's Landing, where they received tents, camp kettles, frying pans, and axes from government-operated stores. They pitched camp beside Lake Superior to await the arrival of another group of 2 officers and 62 men. As soon as the second contingent disembarked, both groups traveled to Lower Fort Garry, about 20 miles north of present-day Winnipeg.

Within days, the temperature dropped to -40°F. On November 3, Lieutenant Colonel W. Osborne Smith, the acting commissioner at Lower Fort Garry, assembled the recruits to take the enlistment oath. They swore to "well and faithfully, diligently and impartially execute and perform such duties as may from time to time be allotted to us." The Northwest Mounted Police (NWMP) was now official.

Steele became a hard-driving sergeant major and fit easily into his role. His job was to turn former clerks, lumberjacks, university students, teachers, farmers, and a bartender into some of the finest horsemen in the world. The recruits slept on raw wooden pallets in ice-cold rooms, only to be awakened at 6:30 A.M. each day by Samuel Steele. One recruit griped that Steele "has no feelings."

In 1873, Lieutenant Colonel W. Osborne Smith swore in Canada's first generation of Mounted Police.

Their buffalo coats, mitts, and moccasins kept the men warm. But the food was bad, and the terrible weather took its toll on some of the recruits. None of them had known exactly what they were getting into when they joined the NWMP. A few of the men resigned from the force, and others were dismissed for drunkenness or for being physically unfit.

By spring 1874, the remaining recruits were disciplined soldiers and accomplished riders. They were fit to face the challenge of the prairies. However, the new commissioner, Colonel George French, recognized that he could not police an area the size of western Europe with a company of only 300 soldiers.

Colonel French returned to Ottawa with an urgent plea to increase the strength of the NWMP. (Steele himself thought the Mounted Police should have at least 1,000 men.) Prime Minister Alexander Mackenzie agreed to double the size of the force, and the colonel spent the rest of the winter in eastern Canada recruiting new men and purchasing horses. On June 6, cheering crowds gathered in Toronto to see off the 217 officers and men and 244 horses traveling to the West in two special railway trains.

The train headed to Dufferin, a village of huts and shops near the U.S. border. Dufferin would be the starting point for the Mounties' march across the plains to the Rocky Mountains. They would take with them all of the provisions and equipment needed to establish posts on the prairies, including livestock to set up food-producing farms. Steele organized the transport, equipment, and provisions for the 80-mile move.

In November 1874, work began on a permanent NWMP post at Fort Saskatchewan. Steele was in charge of laying out the fort and organizing the construction. By the summer of 1875, Fort Saskatchewan was nearly complete. In July, the mail brought welcome news for Steele. He had been appointed regimental sergeant major

Mounties Samuel Steele and Tom Lake appear in this 1875 drawing.

of the force. Steele reported to the headquarters at Swan River and was transferred to Fort Carlton in 1876. There, the government was about to begin negotiations for a treaty with the Cree Indians. At Fort Carlton, Steele and his Mounted Police escorted the government's treaty commissioners. After the treaty was signed, Steele headed to Fort Macleod (in present-day Alberta) to attend official meetings concerning Indian rights and the protection of their land.

When Steele arrived at the fort late in October 1876, he learned from Commissioner J. F. Macleod that the outcome of the Battle of the Little Bighorn that June—in which the Sioux Indians had defeated U.S. soldiers—posed a serious new challenge for the NWMP. General George Custer's defeat had provoked an outcry from U.S. citizens for a final victory over the Sioux. The U.S. Army had orders to seek out and destroy the Sioux, and each skirmish drove the Indians closer to the Canadian border. To prepare for the potentially hostile Indians crossing into Canada, the NWMP had to increase its strength at Fort Macleod.

During the early months of 1877, thousands of Sioux traveled across the border into Canada. Toward the end of May, Sioux chief Sitting Bull—the victor in the Battle of the Little Bighorn—joined them to avoid capture by U.S. soldiers. Sitting Bull, who had great influence over his people, was determined to drive white settlers from Sioux territory in the United States.

Sioux chief Sitting Bull (1834?-1890), who had led the successful attack at the Little Bighorn, tried to prevent white settlers from taking Indian land.

On the morning of September 28, 1877, Steele rode out with Commissioner Macleod to meet with Sitting Bull and the other Sioux chiefs who had fled to Canada. In October, the two sides agreed to peaceful relations, and Sitting Bull chose to return to the United States five years later.

As more settlers arrived in western Canada, the Mounties faced an increase in crime. Life for the Mounted Police at Fort Macleod was a time of endless patrolling on horseback, raiding Indian camps to recover stolen horses and cattle, intercepting outlaws headed for the U.S. border with stolen loot or trying to escape arrest warrants, and arresting whiskey smugglers on their way north through Canada. Steele rose at 6 A.M. and was seldom in bed before midnight.

In February 1881, Canada's Parliament granted the charter for the Canadian Pacific Railway (CPR) to build a rail line across eastern Canada to the Pacific Coast. Steele's job was to ensure that no one interfered with the railway tracks that hundreds of men were laying across 900 miles of prairie.

The NWMP was called in because frontier railway projects attracted thieves, professional gamblers, confidence men, bootleggers, and prostitutes. Also, the Indians

Mounty Samuel Steele spent much of his life protecting Fort Macleod in Alberta.

resented the railway because it would cut through land that had once been theirs and would bring in a flood of white settlers.

Steele pitched his tent at the track-laying headquarters. He decided to control the flow of liquor into the Northwest Territories, where alcohol was not allowed. The thousands of railroad workers still had plenty of opportunities to spend their earnings on alcohol, however, because liquor was available in abundance just across the eastern boundary of the Northwest Territories in Manitoba and in the bordering U.S. states.

As if by magic, shantytowns with gambling dens and brothels sprang up behind the freshly laid track. Steele recognized the impossibility of totally suppressing the liquor traffic, but he made sure that there was never enough liquor at any one place at any time for the workers to go on a drinking spree.

In July 1882, Steele began to oversee the building of the new headquarters of the Mounted Police at the Pile O'Bones settlement. Because there was a shortage of timber on the prairies, manufacturers were constructing pieces of the buildings in eastern Canada and shipping them by rail to the new capital of the western territories, the city of Regina (in present-day Saskatchewan). Steele moved his own headquarters to the nearby Pile O' Bones settlement when the CPR rail had reached that point in September.

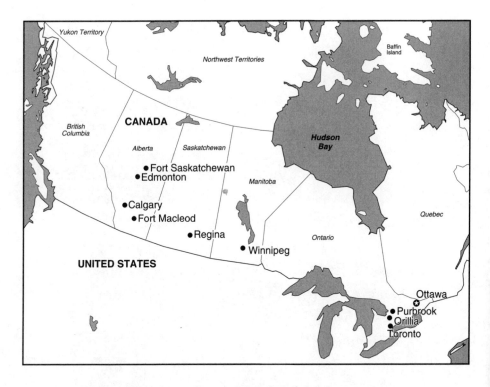

During his career, Samuel Steele left his home town in Ontario to protect the new forts and booming cities in western Canada.

Steele had a triple responsibility: He was in charge of 1) policing the CPR construction, 2) overseeing the construction of the new NWMP headquarters, and 3) supervising police activity in Regina and the disorderly shantytowns that had sprouted up along the freshly laid rail line. This was a tall order, even for Samuel Steele, who had gained a reputation for being the great work-horse of the NWMP.

57

By the spring of 1884, the CPR had finished the comparatively easy construction over the prairies. Now they faced Canada's great mountain barrier, with its sheer rock walls, roaring gorges, and tremendous heights. Moreover, the threat of an avalanche was always present in the winter.

In April 1885, the Canadian Pacific Railroad ran low on money, and unhappy railroad workers grumbled and talked of a strike. Even worse, a band of Cree warriors invaded the tiny village of Frog Lake in the wilderness northeast of Edmonton and massacred nine men, including two mission priests. Taking two widows of the murdered men as hostages, they moved on to besiege the small Mounted Police post at Fort Pitt.

To the east, settlers evacuated Fort Carlton, and a large body of Mounted Police retreated to the town of Prince Albert to protect the civilians who had taken refuge there. Rebellious Indians were in command of the whole eastern half of the Northwest Territories. The possibility also existed that the Blackfoot Indian nation would take up arms against the white settlers living in the west.

Steele arrived in Calgary in April 1885 to find the railway station crammed with frightened families fleeing to Winnipeg. The local Mounted Police had been reduced to a handful of men, and rumors flew that the Blackfoot Indians were preparing to attack the town. However, hostilities ended with little blood spilled as the Indians decided not to test the guns of the Mounties.

Canada's first prime minister, Sir John Alexander Macdonald (1815-1891) described Samuel Steele as Canada's most fearless Mounty. Macdonald held office from 1867 to 1873, and from 1878 to 1891.

The Mounted Police broke the back of the Northwest rebellion on May 12, 1885. As a reward for Steele's long and distinguished service, he was promoted to the rank of superintendent.

In 1889, Steele married Marie Elizabeth Harwood, who had come to Fort Macleod to spend the summer visiting her aunt and uncle, a superintendent at the fort. By January 1898, life at Fort Macleod had grown comfortable for Superintendent Steele, and he was looking forward to another year of more or less routine service. But a telegram on January 29 ordered him to the Yukon. Leaving behind his wife and children, Steele took command of the town of Dawson, which had swollen in size because of prospectors looking for gold in that area.

But the settlement at Dawson lacked the stability that Steele had created at Fort Macleod. Heavy flooding during the spring and summer had turned the town site into one vast sewer and caused an epidemic of typhoid fever. In addition, saloons, gambling dens, and brothels had sprung up all over the new town. As Steele began to bring law and order to the Yukon, he expanded the jails throughout the area. By the autumn of 1898, he had overseen the construction of 63 new buildings at the Mounties' 20 Yukon posts.

In 1899, Steele began another new adventure. After years of bickering about the large number of British prospectors moving into the colony of South Africa, the descendants of Dutch emigrants living there (the *Boers*) went to war with the British government running the colony. A reluctant Canadian government sent a Canadian contingent thousands of miles across the globe to support the British. The Mounted Police offered a highly trained force of officers, as well as the ideal leader for the expedition to South Africa—Lieutenant Colonel Samuel Steele. Steele volunteered for service in South Africa with the understanding that he would remain an officer of Canada's Northwest Mounted Police.

On January 25, 1900, Steele received a telegram from the Canadian government, offering him command of an entirely new unit. This would be a special corps of mounted riflemen from western Canada, built around a core of officers from the Mounted Police.

Steele spent several years in South Africa, first fighting the Boers and then helping to establish peace in the country. The British people and government never forgot his service to them during the Boer War.

After leaving South Africa, Steele and his family traveled to Great Britain. There, he held the position of acting adjutant general to the inspector general of cavalry for the British Army. Steele studied military science in preparation for yet another troubleshooting assignment: He was asked to build up western Canada's military for the anticipated war with Germany. By now, the Mounted Police had been renamed the Royal Northwest Mounted Police, and Samuel Steele had become the best-known and most respected soldier in Canada.

In 1914, Steele was in Winnipeg commanding Military District Number 10, which stretched from the Great Lakes to the eastern boundary of Alberta. In the years since leaving South Africa, he had strengthened Canada's military forces. Enlistments in his district had increased 600 percent. At age 63, Steele was perfectly capable of leading the Expeditionary Force that Canada was sending to Europe as World War I began. He seemed like the very man to inspire young Canadians to enlist and to then infuse them with high morale when they got to the front.

The Canadian government soon promoted Steele to major general, the highest rank then held by a Canadian Mounty. With the new promotion, Steele became inspector general in charge of training all the land forces from the Great Lakes to the Pacific. When the government announced Steele's appointment, he received a flood of congratulatory messages. The appointment was extremely popular in western Canada, where people considered Steele their hero.

Within two months, Steele organized a complete division of 25,000 men. When Steele, along with his wife and their children, arrived in Great Britain, they moved into a house in Folkestone, near the Canadian camp. In 1916, a Canadian commander who had been stationed in France became Steele's supervisor. This new commanding officer thought that Steele no longer had the energy necessary to do his job. On December 1, the Canadian government terminated Steele's command. Canadian officials wanted someone else to lead their troops into battle in World War I.

Even though Steele continued to work in Canada's War Office in Britain, the Canadian authorities treated him poorly, ignoring his decisions wherever they could. The Canadian officials thought that Steele was becoming too ambivalent about his work, and they put him on the retired list as of July 1, 1918.

Later that year, in recognition of Steele's nearly 50 years of service to Canada and Great Britain, the British Home Forces Command officially knighted him. Steele was pleased with this rare honor, but the fact that a similar honor had not come from his own country hurt him.

On November 11, 1918, the First World War ended. The Steeles celebrated the event quietly at home. There would be no transportation back to Canada for some time for the retired general and his family. All available space on shipboard would be filled by returning front-line troops. As he waited in England, Steele began to make plans for his return to Canada. He had been offered directorships in several Canadian companies, and he saw an active life ahead of him—even if his career with the Mounties had ended. Steele wished to return to western Canada, the scene of his greatest happiness.

A widespread influenza epidemic struck England in 1918 and 1919. Although Steele had often survived such outbreaks in his younger years, he did not survive this one. Samuel Steele died in Putney, England, in the early hours of January 30, 1919.

Steele's funeral procession, which was held two days later, was like a pageant of his life. His coffin was covered with the the British flag and carried in procession at a gun carriage. Behind the carriage came a troop of red-coated Mounted Police from the force that had served on the European front during World War I. Behind them rode members of the detachment Steele had commanded in South Africa. Then came files of men from the Second Canadian Division—the infantry soldiers, gunners, signalers, cooks, dentists, and paymasters from the fighting machine that he had built and sent off to war.

Steele had requested to be buried in Winnipeg, Canada. His body arrived there one day in the middle of the general strike of 1919. Riots raged on Main Street, and the several Mounties called in to restore order were badly beaten up.

The rioting continued into the evening. The strike was still in progress the next morning, when the largest funeral procession western Canada had ever seen was held. Strikers lined the streets as Steele's casket passed by. Mounted Police rode behind the riderless black horse with Steele's boots reversed in the stirrups. Even after his death, Sam Steele was bringing order to a disorderly world.

In 1920, the Mounties changed their official name to the Royal Canadian Mounted Police (RCMP). The Mounties now enforce federal law throughout Canada, and they are the only law enforcement officers in Canada's Northwest and Yukon territories. Steele would hardly recognize today's Mounted Police.

The present-day RCMP is a member of the International Criminal Police Organization (Interpol).

Canadian Mounties (shown here around the year 1920) have been a proud tradition in Canada's history. Today, nearly 20,000 men and women are members of the Royal Canadian Mounted Police.

The Mounties now have extensive crime-detection laboratories and identification branches that are available to all authorized police forces worldwide. Selected members of the force attend an RCMP-sponsored Canadian Police College. Yet with of all its technological changes, Steele's high standards are still at the heart of the organization he did so much to establish.

Though sometimes impulsive in his pursuit of justice, Captain Leander H. McNelly (1844-1877) turned the Texas Rangers into a respected crime fighting unit during the 1870s.

4

Leander H. McNelly
Captain of the Texas Rangers

*O*f all the law-enforcement organizations in history, the Texas Rangers have probably changed the most over time. In fact, the Rangers seldom fought crime in an organized fashion until the 1870s, when Leander H. McNelly came along. A sickly officer who sometimes had to direct his men from a wagon bed, McNelly was nonetheless one of the most fearless of all the Texas Rangers. He was cool under pressure and won the respect of his men. Because of his accomplishments, he has sometimes been called the *last* of the great Texas Rangers.

The Texas Rangers were first organized in 1835 during the Texas Revolution, when the territory won its independence from Mexico. (Texas, however, did not officially join the United States until 1845.) The Rangers had no uniforms and were often known for their recklessness. Although they seldom numbered more than 500 men, the Rangers were Texas's primary law officers throughout much of the nineteenth century.

From 1846 to 1848, the Rangers served as scouts and fighters during the Mexican War, and during the 1850s, they carried out vicious battles against the Comanche Indians. After the Civil War, however, the U.S. Cavalry began to handle many of the Indian conflicts on the western frontier, leaving the Rangers more time to pursue bank robbers and cattle rustlers.

By the 1870s, when Leander H. McNelly joined the Texas Rangers, the force began to focus most of its attention on fighting crime. McNelly, who was born in 1844, had already led an exciting life. Before joining the Texas Rangers, he had been a captain in the Confederate Army during the Civil War, an officer with the Texas State Police, and a Methodist preacher.

In the spring of 1874, when McNelly was 30, a group of Rangers reporting to him went to DeWitt County to help settle a bloody feud between the Sutton and Taylor families, who often broke laws while seeking revenge on each other. On March 11, William Taylor—of the Taylor clan—and an unknown accomplice boarded

"Ride like Mexicans, shoot like Tennesseans, and fight like the devil" was the motto for the Texas Rangers.

a steamboat that was docked at Indianola in eastern Texas and murdered two passengers who were members of the Sutton clan. Texas police arrested Taylor in early April. Taylor would be held in Galveston until shortly before his trial, which was scheduled to begin in Indianola on September 24.

Texas Ranger general William Steele asked Captain McNelly to come to Indianola and ensure a safe trial for

William Taylor, who might easily be murdered by a vindictive member of the Sutton clan.

On September 19, General Steele telegraphed McNelly to report to Indianola on the day before the trial. Unfortunately, because the heavy rains and the swollen streams cut off the mail, no one could deliver the telegram until four days after the trial was scheduled to begin. McNelly was busy handling other cases at the time, so he sent several of his officers to Indianola without him. In the meantime, the Sutton clan was planning to go to Indianola to ensure their own kind of justice.

To protect Taylor, Governor Richard Coke ordered General Steele to Galveston. There, Steele led a group of

Officials in Washington, D.C., had their doubts about the effectiveness of the Texas Rangers. But Texas governor Richard Coke, who held office from 1874 to 1876, gave the Rangers his full support.

soldiers who escorted the prisoner by steamboat to Indianola for trial. When they arrived at Indianola on September 23, the Rangers marched the prisoner to the jail in the midst of a squad of soldiers. Angry mobs planned to attack Taylor while he was in court, but the presence of McNelly's Rangers prevented any disturbance at the trial.

The Texas Rangers did not confine their activities to guarding prisoners and protecting courts. McNelly established a spy network and sent scouting expeditions all over the country in search of troublemakers. When he heard that John Wesley Hardin and fellow outlaws would be in DeWitt County, he told his men he would rather kill all his horses than let Hardin escape from their custody. He sent squads of four to six men to scout the countryside for Hardin, but they did not find him.

Early in November 1874, a United States marshal from Galveston requested that McNelly aid him in serving 27 warrants for the capture of outlaw Joe Tumlinson, a friend of the Sutton family. At the end of November, Captain McNelly made a lengthy report covering his stay in DeWitt County. In his report he stated that the presence of the Texas Rangers there had been beneficial and their conduct good. He said that the peaceful citizens in the county considered the Rangers an absolute necessity, and added that trouble would break out immediately upon their removal.

Life in DeWitt County had become more secure for the settlers there because the Rangers had instilled fear in the hearts of outlaws. But even the Rangers could not heal the deep wounds that the Sutton-Taylor feud had made.

During this period, the Texas legislature divided the Rangers into two divisions. In 1874, the Frontier Battalion was formed to deal with Indian conflicts in the western part of the state. The Batallion, which was commanded by Major John B. Jones, had six companies of 75 men each. In the spring of 1875, Texas officials asked Captain McNelly to organize the Special Force of the Texas Rangers. This smaller, elite force would be sent to southwest Texas to suppress the growing number of bandit raids along the Mexican border. McNelly began recruiting in April, and had more than 40 Rangers by the month's end.

One of McNelly's first priorities was to change the Rangers' reputation for lawlessness. He told his men they couldn't arrest people without evidence they had done something wrong. Nor should the Rangers steal food from people's gardens or shoot dogs just because they were barking too loud. McNelly also hoped to curb the number of vigilante posses, which sometimes caused as much trouble as the criminals they were trying to apprehend.

Although he may have had a softer heart than some of the previous Rangers, McNelly was still harsh. He

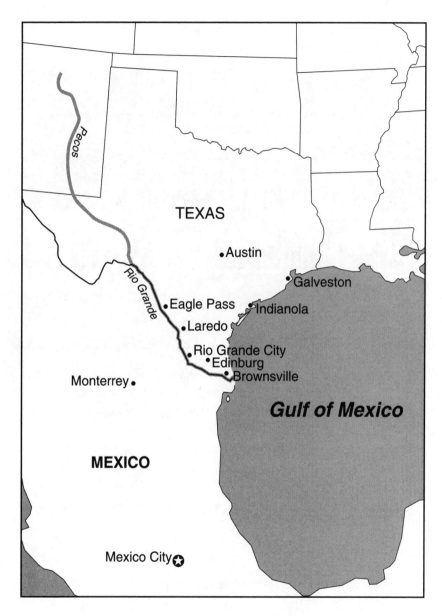

The Special Force of the Texas Rangers, led by Captain Leander H. McNelly, protected cities in the southern part of the state from cattle thieves and desperados.

READ AND REFLECT!

In view of the fact that CRIME has run riot to such an alarming extent in the Territory of Montana, (particularly East of the Missouri River,) during the past six months, and that

Murders and High-handed Outrages

Have been of such frequent occurrence as to excite the just indignation of all good citizens, it is believed that it is now time that the GOOD WORK should be re-commenced. Therefore,

THIS IS TO NOTIFY ALL WHOM IT MAY CONCERN!

That CRIME MUST AND WILL BE SUPPRESSED! and to that end, all OFFENDERS

WILL BE SUMMARILY DEALT WITH!

AND PUNISHED AS OF OLD!

BY ORDER OF

VIGILANCE COMMITTEE.

As shown in this notice from the late 1800s, many Americans grew tired of lawlessness on the western frontier and were willing to form vigilante groups to curb crime.

instituted the practice of *la ley de fuga* (Spanish for "the law regarding escape"), which meant any prisoner caught trying to escape would be executed. During his career, McNelly killed a few escaping prisoners, even though some of the Rangers thought this punishment was too harsh. McNelly used his experience as a Methodist preacher to conduct funeral services for the dead prisoners before dumping their bodies in the middle of town.

On April 18, 1875, General Steele received the following telegram from Sheriff John McClure of Nueces County: "Is Capt. McNelly coming? We are in trouble. Five ranches burned by disguised men near Laparra last week. Answer."

As Captain McNelly approached the U.S.-Mexican border, he found the countryside overrun by bands of armed men. McNelly described the situation the following way:

> The acts committed by Americans [against Mexicans] are horrible to relate. Many ranches have been plundered and burned, and the people murdered or driven away. One of these parties confessed to me . . . as having killed 11 men on their last raid. I immediately issued an order disbanding the minute companies and all armed bands acting without the authority of the state. My order was obeyed, or agreed to be, without hesitation. Had I not disbanded these companies, it is possible and very probable that civil war would have ensued as the Mexicans are very much exasperated.

In the latter part of May, McNelly moved to Brownsville, where he planned to remain through June. The residents of Brownsville were very much alarmed about their safety because the commander at nearby Fort Brown reported that countless thieves from Mexico had been freely crossing over into Texas and that he had only 150 officers to defend the area. Mexican ranchers had

Because herds could easily be resold for large profits, ranches in the American southwest were often pillaged by cattle thieves during the 1800s.

received large contracts to deliver beef to businesses in Cuba. The success of well-known Mexican cattle thief Juan Cortinas had inspired numerous other Mexicans to steal cattle as well.

When McNelly reached Brownsville, a steam boat sat three miles offshore to receive a herd of 400 cattle that was being held in Mexico. Cortinas himself was in the area with 75 men, half of whom were mounted on horses with U.S. brands. McNelly knew immediately that Cortinas had come to Texas to steal more cattle.

From June through October that year, McNelly spent his time fighting the persistent problem of cattle thieves. He instituted an effective spy system, and on many occasions learned of the thieves' plans in time to foil them. McNelly and his men engaged the outlaws in a battle and recaptured the cattle. After apprehending and killing bandits on Palo Alto Prairie—the site of the first battle during the Mexican War—the Rangers had made the Mexicans very careful not to be caught. Mexican thieves no longer hesitated to abandon their stolen goods and escape from McNelly and his men.

Although McNelly had a strong spirit, he was often ill. After experiencing severe chills and a high fever toward the beginning of October 1875, Captain McNelly went home to Washington County. When he returned to duty later that month, he learned that approximately 250 head of cattle had been stolen from Cameron County.

On November 12, McNelly discovered that the men who had purchased stolen cattle were staying at the Las Cuevas ranch, located three miles across the U.S.-Mexican border. The thieves were under contract to deliver the cattle to Monterrey, Mexico, within 90 days.

McNelly contacted federal officials in Washington, D.C., telling them he planned to attack the ranch and force the Mexicans to return the stolen cattle. He also asked the U.S. Army to to meet him near the Rio Grande (Spanish for *large river*), which separates Texas from

Mexico, to help the Rangers apprehend the rustlers and bring the cattle back to Texas.

Before hearing from Washington, McNelly led a group of 30 Texas Rangers over the Rio Grande and into Mexico. When they approached the Las Cuevas ranch, the Rangers saw approximately 250 Mexican men on horseback dash into the ranch. The Rangers opened fire at the small group of armed Mexicans who approached them. General Juan Flores, who owned the ranch, fell dead. The Rangers also killed about eight other Mexican men, though they could not be certain they were all cattle thieves.

After the initial victory—later known as the Battle of Las Cuevas—McNelly reassessed the situation. Because he had only 30 men with him, charging the ranch house would be suicide. Instead, McNelly decided to go back to Texas, hoping that federal troops would arrive.

McNelly's request for federal reinforcements was met on November 19, when army captain John F. Randlett and about 40 U.S. soldiers arrived at the Rio Grande to reinforce the Rangers. But McNelly could not persuade Randlett and his men to walk more than a few steps into Mexico. Army major A. J. Alexander had sent Randlett a telegram saying, "If McNelly is attacked by Mexican forces on Mexican soil, do not render him any assistance." Therefore, Randlett would only help McNelly if he was attacked in Texas or on the Mexican border.

When the Rangers learned that 200 Mexican soldiers and representatives from the Mexican government had arrived at the ranch, McNelly decided to return to Texas. But just as he made that decision, a messenger handed them a neatly written document from the Mexican government, which asked that the U.S. soldiers leave Mexico. Randlett and his men immediately returned to the Texas side of the border.

McNelly stayed in Mexico, however, and had a telegram sent to Major Alexander, requesting that he order the Army soldiers back into Mexico. McNelly and his men camped on Mexican soil—just over the U.S.-Mexican border—waiting to hear if Alexander had changed his mind. As night fell, the Rangers held their position and dug trenches and prepared for the Mexicans to attack.

On November 20, McNelly announced that he would attack the Mexican army if the stolen cattle was not returned. After a few moments of consultation, the Mexican officials agreed to deliver all 250 head of stolen cattle to Rio Grande City the following day. McNelly, however, demanded that the Mexicans deliver the cattle to the Texas side of the Rio Grande. Though he knew that the U.S. Army was unwilling to help him, McNelly told the Mexican authorities that U.S. forces were prepared to assist the Rangers in attacking Mexico if the cattle were not returned on time. After considering

McNelly's message, the Mexican officials said they agreed to his demands. McNelly's bluff had worked.

The following afternoon, McNelly took 10 men up to Rio Grande City to get the stolen cattle. When the cattle arrived at 4 P.M., the herd was delivered to the Mexican side of the river, not in Texas as McNelly had insisted. Using a messenger, Captain McNelly told the Mexican officials to bring the cattle over the Rio Grande into Texas. The Mexicans sent word back that they could not deliver the cattle until they had been inspected by the Texans.

There were 25 Mexicans with the cattle and 10 Rangers. The Rangers crossed the Rio Grande and found that the Mexicans had only 76 of the 250 cattle that had been stolen. (They had been unable to locate the remaining missing cattle.) Even worse, a representative from the Mexican government said he could not return the cattle until they had been inspected.

McNelly ordered his men to fall in rank. They instantly loaded their guns and prepared to fire. When the messenger told the Mexicans that the Rangers would kill all of them if they didn't deliver the cattle across the river in less than five minutes, the Mexicans immediately did as they were told. Although McNelly was adamant that his men not infringe upon the rights of innocent people, McNelly didn't mind threatening people whom he felt were being dishonest.

In March 1876, Captain McNelly learned that more stolen cattle were being driven north from southern Texas to Kansas. According to local rumors, the cattle thieves had hired the infamous John Wesley Hardin to keep competitors out of the Devil's River area, where many thieves took refuge. If this was so, McNelly had an opportunity to rid the state of Hardin, who had become one of the most feared outlaws in the Southwest.

But matters occurring on the Rio Grande made the Devil's River expedition impossible. Mexico was in turmoil, as General Porfiorio Diaz had made himself a dictator. In the middle of April, McNelly discovered that General Diaz was working with the Mexican cattle thieves. On April 25, McNelly heard that Diaz was

John Wesley Hardin (1853-1895), who murdered at least 37 people, studied law from his prison cell until his 1894 release—then worked as an attorney until an angry police officer shot him dead the following year.

81

One of McNelly's contemporaries, Captain James B. Gillett, wrote about the Rangers' capture of John Wesley Hardin and other outlaws in his 1921 book, Six Years with the Texas Rangers.

forcing men into his service, and many were crossing into Texas to avoid working for him.

In May, Captain McNelly received news that there would be a cattle raid near the town of Laredo, and that 500 head of cattle would be driven across the border into Mexico. On the night of May 17, McNelly followed a gang of about nine raiders to the river at a point five miles upstream from Edinburg. By the time they reached the river, the Mexicans had succeeded in crossing all of the cattle.

McNelly sent a note to Captain H. J. Farnsworth of the Eighth U.S. Cavalry, which was stationed in Edinburg. McNelly asked Farnsworth to assist in recapturing the cattle. Farnsworth arrived the following morning with 50 men, but he said he would assist McNelly in recrossing the river only if he believed the Rangers would be unable to get back to Texas without his help. Some of McNelly's guides thought that a part of the cattle were at the nearby Sabinisto Ranch. McNelly and his men crossed the river and went into Mexico once more to locate stolen cattle.

McNelly told the Mexican officials about the affair and asked for the return of the stolen cattle as soon as they could be found. The Mexican government promised to return the cattle. On May 31, McNelly wrote from Laredo that he was leaving for the Nueces region in Mexico, where he hoped to catch a gang of 20 or 25 men. He would break his company into small squads and then scout the area for thieves.

On June 4, McNelly captured cattle thief King Fisher and nine of his men. He took them to Eagle Pass. But the local authorities turned the men loose. They said there was not enough evidence to hold the men, despite the fact that seven of them were suspected of murder. McNelly had, however, recovered the 500 head of stolen cattle, even though the culprits were released from custody.

Soon afterward, McNelly went to Austin, where dozens of King Fisher's men had reportedly begun stealing property in daylight. The residents were too afraid to fight back against the robbers or attempt to reclaim their belongings. The local authorities were outnumbered and felt powerless to confront the thieves. Terror was spreading, and several of the settlers declared that they had not suffered half as much from the Indians as they had from the outlaws.

McNelly's officers quickly spotted some of Fisher's bandits and apprehended them, even though the Rangers themselves hadn't witnessed the men commit any crimes. But Fisher had a lawyer, who reminded McNelly that the courts now required that law officers must have legal evidence before throwing someone in jail, and Fisher's men were released. (The residents of Austin who had witnessed the thefts had been too afraid of the criminals to press charges.) Frustrated and unable to curb the crime problem in the city, McNelly came to the conclusion that virtually all white residents in the area were outlaws working for King Fisher.

Conditions were even worse in Goliad, where the large cattle owners had formed a company of "regulators" to scare off or kill people who weren't property owners. On the night of August 28, the former sheriff of San Patricio County, who was living in the town, was killed while in the doorway of a local church. Before one of McNelly's Rangers could arrive to investigate,

A group of Texas Rangers relax at their camp in Menard County during the 1870s.

however, the coroner had decided that there was not enough evidence to arrest anyone for murder. Many people believed the murderer was hired by one of the "regulators." However, because the ranchers hired strangers from out of town to do their killing, no one could be certain who the murderer was or why the sheriff and others had been killed. Such obstacles frustrated McNelly, because he had learned that they were part of the job.

McNelly's last recorded mission as a Texas Ranger was made in October. At that time, he and five of his men went to Clinton for the purpose of escorting five members of the notorious Sutton clan to the Galveston jail. McNelly then became too ill for further service at this point, and General William Steele relieved him of duty. Lee Hall, who had served as a second lieutenant under McNelly, was made captain in his place. The result was widespread criticism from the Texas press, since people across the state had grown fond of McNelly.

To defend his actions, General Steele said that McNelly's medical expenses constituted one-third of the medical bill for his entire company of Rangers. Steele commended Hall for being "in the full vigor of early manhood and health" and said that the Rangers were much more economical without McNelly.

Despite public support, the man who had tried so hard to bring peace and security to southern Texas was forced into an early retirement. McNelly became very ill with tuberculosis soon afterward. He died in Burton on September 4, 1877, at the age of 33.

In the decades that followed, McNelly's successors continued his tradition of fighting crime in Texas. Lee Hall, in fact, became the first person to distribute badges to the Texas Rangers. During the early twentieth century, however, the Rangers' law-enforcement responsibilities gradually began to diminish. In 1935, the Texas legislature voted to merge the Rangers with the state highway patrol.

Four Texas Rangers, shown here during the 1890s. From left to right: Bob Speaker, Lon Odom, Jim Putman, and Captain John R. Hughes.

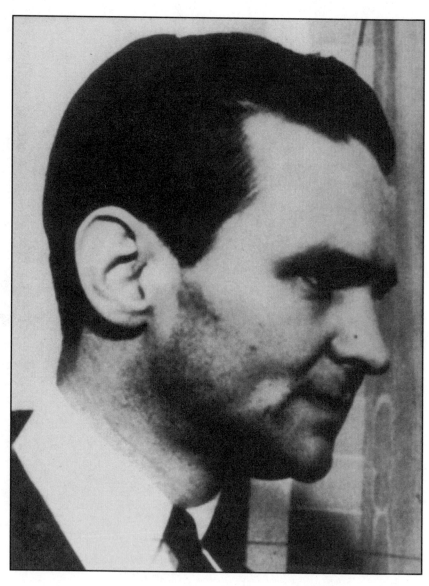

Federal agent Melvin Purvis (1903-1960) became famous through his highly publicized campaign to track down John Dillinger.

5

Melvin Purvis and Eliot Ness
Top Agents of the FBI

*T*wo of the most famous agents in the history of the Federal Bureau of Investigation (FBI), Melvin Purvis and Eliot Ness, gained national attention during the 1920s and 1930s while pursuing the most wanted criminals in the United States.

Purvis's unorthodox methods and craving for the limelight sometimes angered his boss, J. Edgar Hoover. Eliot Ness, on the other hand, became an American legend after his exploits battling "the mob," a term that many people used to describe organized crime.

The FBI was created in 1908 as the Bureau of Investigation of the U.S. Department of Justice. The bureau was established to investigate violations of federal law and matters that might affect U.S. interests. The FBI (as it would be called beginning in 1935) investigated espionage, sabotage, subversive activities, and other actions related to national security.

Following its reorganization in 1924, J. Edgar Hoover became the bureau's director and established its policies. Hoover, who had worked for the Justice Department since 1917, now reported directly to the U.S. attorney general. During his years with the Bureau of Investigation, Hoover had compiled a vast fingerprint file from thousands of arrest fingerprints that had been acquired from the federal penitentiary at Leavenworth, Kansas, and the International Association of Chiefs of Police. As local and state law enforcement agencies throughout the United States forwarded fingerprint records to the FBI, its criminal identification data increased. Hoover also pushed for a crime laboratory and a training academy.

During the Great Depression of the 1930s, organized crime threatened U.S. society. Fighting organized crime became a priority for the FBI, and Hoover put some of his best men on the job of breaking up the criminal organizations. He selected his agents from a national pool of officers. Applicants had to be between 23 and 40 years of age. In addition, they needed to have a degree

Over the past 100 years, the federal penitentiary in Leavenworth, Kansas, has housed some of the most notorious outlaws in U.S. history.

from a state-accredited law school or be graduates of a four-year college with an accounting major and at least three years of work experience in law enforcement.

Melvin Purvis more than measured up to these standards; he captured more public enemies than any other federal agent. Purvis directed hunts that netted such infamous gangsters as Lester Gillis (known as "Baby Face Nelson") and Charles "Pretty Boy" Floyd. He won great acclaim as the man who set the trap for John Dillinger, one of America's most notorious criminals.

Born in 1903, Purvis was raised in the farming community of Timmonsville, South Carolina. He earned a law degree from the University of South Carolina, then worked as an attorney for a law firm in Florence, South

J. Edgar Hoover (1895-1972) served as head of the FBI under eight presidents, starting with Calvin Coolidge and ending with Richard Nixon.

Carolina. He joined the Department of Justice in 1927 and served in the bureau's field office in Dallas, Texas, before Hoover assigned him to the Chicago office. Soon Purvis's name began appearing in newspapers. Neither quiet nor unassuming, Purvis loved the spotlight and enjoyed the attention he received from the Chicago press.

Purvis came to Chicago at a time when gangsters were making their names known throughout the Midwest. On one of his first assignments, Purvis arrested Roger Touhy and three of his henchmen for kidnapping millionaire brewer William Hamm of St. Paul, Minnesota, in 1933, but a jury found the gang not guilty. Later, authorities discovered that the Hamm job was the work of the Barker-Karpis gang, led by Alvin "Creepy" Karpis and

Ma Barker and her sons. At that time, Karpis was the Bureau of Investigation's "public enemy number one."

Immediately after Touhy's trial, Purvis charged Touhy and his men with kidnapping the son of Jake "the Barber" Factor, a mysterious underworld figure who was wanted in Great Britain. Because of Factor's criminal connections, some people were not sure whether Factor's son had really been kidnapped. Nevertheless, a court found Touhy guilty and sentenced him to a lengthy prison sentence.

In 1934, Purvis took on his most famous assignment: to apprehend John Dillinger. Dillinger, who was born in Indianapolis in 1903, joined the Dirty Dozen gang as a youth. But he did not become involved in serious crime until 1924 after serving briefly in the navy. That year, Dillinger and an older criminal attempted to rob a grocer whom they knew usually carried the day's receipts on him. The two men accosted their victim on a dark street. Dillinger struck the grocer on the head with a gun wrapped in a handkerchief. The grocer struggled, and Dillinger ran off without a cent. He was arrested almost immediately afterward.

The local prosecuting attorney assured Dillinger that as a first-time offender he would be treated lightly if he pleaded guilty. Instead, John Dillinger ended up serving nine years in prison. Meanwhile, his accomplice—who was about ten years older than Dillinger—served only two years. The difference in sentencing and the

The U.S. Department of Justice building, which houses the FBI's central headquarters, as it looked during the 1930s

experience in captivity made Dillinger bitter and resentful. First he served time in the Indiana State Reformatory, then was moved to the state prison at Michigan City. In prison, Dillinger came in contact with criminals who became his mentors and later his accomplices.

When the state released Dillinger from prison in May 1933, he immediately set about committing robberies to raise the funds he needed to arrange a mass escape of his cohorts still behind bars. He badly bungled his first robberies, but finally managed to steal $10,600 from a bank. Then he pulled off a payroll heist that yielded more than $24,000. He now had enough funds to bribe the prison guards and "spring" his friends.

Once in action, Dillinger and company robbed at least ten banks within eight months. In January 1934, the gang moved to Tucson, Arizona. There, the authorities captured Dillinger and flew him to Chicago. His plane was met by 85 police officers, and a 13-car convoy then took America's most famous prisoner to an "escape-proof" jail in Crown Point, Indiana.

Two months later, Dillinger electrified the nation with his famous "wooden gun" prison escape. According to the popular version of this story, Dillinger made his "gun" by whittling the top of a wooden washboard and coloring it with shoe polish. The *true* story was that Dillinger's lawyer smuggled him a *real* gun. Dillinger used the gun to capture and lock up several guards, and then made his escape. The "wooden-gun" story was widely reported by the U.S. press, nevertheless, and Dillinger was on his way to becoming a national symbol of lawlessness.

After escaping from prison in March 1934, Dillinger immediately put together another gang, which included Lester Gillis, who was better known as "Baby Face Nelson." The Dillinger gang moved throughout the Midwest. Illinois and Indiana had special "Dillinger Squads" to try to track down the outlaw, and newspapers

During the Great Depression, Americans intensely followed the exploits of "public enemy" John Dillinger, who killed at least 10 people during his criminal career.

called Dillinger the modern version of nineteenth-century bank robber Jesse James.

The Dillinger gang had become a thorn in the side of J. Edgar Hoover. Not only was Dillinger a tenacious outlaw, but all the publicity he received was making Hoover and his agents look bad. Hoover didn't have to wait long for the opportunity to go after Dillinger. Following his escape from Crown Point, Dillinger stole a local sheriff's car and drove it from Indiana to Illinois. Transporting a stolen car across state lines was a federal offense that fell under the jurisdiction of the FBI. Now Hoover made Dillinger "public enemy number one" and assigned Purvis to capture or kill the bandit.

By this time, agent Purvis had developed a reckless approach to investigating lawbreakers. He and his men in Chicago took their techniques of grilling suspects from gangster films, which had become popular among movie audiences during the early 1930s. In an effort to make their prisoners confess, the agents sometimes dangled them by their hands out of 17-story windows.

In April 1934, Purvis received a tip that the Dillinger gang was hiding out at the Little Bohemia Lodge in northern Wisconsin. Purvis and other federal agents flew northward in several small planes and landed at Rhinelander, Wisconsin. Meanwhile, in Washington, D.C., Hoover called a press conference to announce that Dillinger was surrounded and couldn't possibly escape.

Commandeering several cars, the agents drove to the lodge and recklessly fired at the first three men who stepped from the premises. They killed one man and wounded another. But these men had been regular guests at the lodge—not criminals! Because of this fiasco, the Justice Department almost decided to demote Hoover and discharge Purvis. By now, newspapers were calling Dillinger names like the "human cobra" because of his knack for slithering away. Over the past year, he had

97

stolen $265,000, and the government seemed no closer to apprehending him.

Desperate to make up for the Little Bohemia disaster, Purvis pursued every possibility of getting Dillinger. In June 1934, Martin Zarkovich, a police sergeant from East Chicago, approached Purvis. Zarkovich claimed that Dillinger could be captured with the help of Anna Sage. Sage, with her own criminal record to worry about, agreed to help Purvis catch Dillinger. Their plan called for setting a trap outside a Chicago movie house on July 22, 1934. Purvis told his agents, "Gentlemen, you know the character of John Dillinger. If . . . we locate him and he makes an escape, it will be a disgrace to our bureau."

When Dillinger left the movie house at 6 P.M., Purvis called out, "Stick 'em up, Johnny, we've got you surrounded!" As Dillinger reached for his gun, the federal agents shot him to death. Following the shooting, the press praised Purvis as the killer of John Dillinger, and he received the heartfelt thanks of his boss, J. Edgar Hoover—and many bank presidents.

On October 22, 1934, Purvis, again following a tip, cornered Charles "Pretty Boy" Floyd, whom Hoover had identified as the machine gun killer in the 1933 "Kansas City Massacre" of five law officers. Purvis found Floyd hiding at a farm outside of East Liverpool, Ohio. When Purvis demanded to knew whether Floyd was responsible for the massacre in Kansas City, the crook denied having been there and tried to escape. Purvis

After his days as a bank robber came to an end, John Dillinger was buried in the Crown Hill cemetery in Indianapolis, Indiana.

then turned to another agent and ordered him to shoot Floyd to death, which he did.

By this time, Purvis had helped to capture more wanted criminals than any other FBI agent. That year, *Literary Digest* published a readers' survey that ranked Purvis eighth in a list of the year's outstanding world figures. He came in ahead of North Pole explorer Admiral Richard Byrd and Secretary of Labor Frances Perkins, the first woman to serve in a president's cabinet.

The *New York Evening Journal's* headline read, "And Again Melvin Purvis Triumphs." The *New York Times* hailed Purvis as *the* nemesis of public enemies.

By 1935, Hoover's attitude toward Purvis had changed radically because Purvis was grabbing headlines that Hoover thought should have gone to the FBI as a whole or to Hoover himself. Hoover was also envious of Attorney General Homer Cummings, who received much of the credit for the success of the FBI agents—or "G-Men," as they were sometimes called—even though

Gangster George "Machine Gun" Kelly is credited for coining the term "G-Men"—short for "government men"—to describe Hoover's federal agents.

Hoover was overseeing the FBI's day-to-day operations. The FBI director assigned several agents to spy on Purvis, and Hoover harassed Purvis about his conduct and procedures so often that the agent finally resigned from the bureau later that year.

Purvis attempted to get several jobs with corporations, but Hoover interfered. When Purvis was about to be hired in Hollywood as an adviser on FBI activities and procedures, Hoover contacted all the Hollywood directors and told them that he would not look kindly upon their employing Purvis. At that time, Hoover was so influential that no one in Hollywood would hire the former agent.

When Purvis applied for a position as security chief at the Santa Anita Racetrack, Clyde Tolson—one of Hoover's top lieutenants—contacted the directors of the track and told them not to hire Purvis. Purvis, of course, didn't get the job. In 1936, however, Purvis was hired as an announcer for the "Junior G-Men" children's radio show. The following year, he narrated a radio show sponsored by the Post Toasties breakfast cereal and commanded Inspector Post's Junior Detective Corps, which was later renamed the Melvin Purvis Law and Order Patrol.

During World War II, Purvis worked for the War Crimes Section of the U.S. Army's judge advocate general. But Hoover continued to snipe at him. On February 29, 1960, after several business ventures had failed, Purvis shot himself to death.

While Purvis was becoming famous for nabbing big-name criminals, Eliot Ness and other FBI agents were working feverishly to stop a bigger monster—organized crime. As the term implies, some criminals began applying tried-and-true business strategies to their illegal endeavors.

Ironically, a federal law gave organized crime the boost it needed to succeed. When the Eighteenth Amendment took effect in January 1920, the era of Prohibition began. Prohibition made the manufacture and sale of alcoholic beverages illegal, but the law was unpopular with many Americans. Many criminals saw Prohibition as an opportunity to make huge profits by manufacturing and distributing alcoholic beverages, and illegal saloons—known as *speakeasies*—soon sprang up across the nation.

Financed by massive profits, organized crime began taking over entire cities. Members of the "mob" bribed politicians and police officers, threatened honest business owners, and encouraged lawlessness wherever they went. Something had to be done, and the Bureau of Investigation was called upon to stop organized crime from spreading any further.

As head of the so-called "Untouchables," Eliot Ness became one of the most famous law officers in American history. More than any other group, his band of FBI agents helped break the stranglehold that Al Capone and his mob had on Chicago and the nation.

These scenes during Prohibition show federal agents finding a hidden alcohol still and pouring bottles of "bootleg" liquor into the street.

Eliot Ness was born in Chicago in 1902. As a teenager, he was an avid reader of Sherlock Holmes mysteries and dreamed of becoming a detective. After graduating from the University of Chicago in 1925 with a bachelor's degree in commerce and business administration, Ness found a job as an investigator for the Retail Credit Company. From there he moved to the Prohibition Bureau of the U.S. Department of Justice.

In 1928, Hoover placed Ness in charge of a Prohibition detail that had been specifically created to put Al Capone out of business. At the time, Capone was becoming an international symbol for crime in the United States. Ness weeded through hundreds of files before he came up with the names of nine Bureau of Investigation agents who seemed so trustworthy that Ness did not think even the powerful Capone gang could blackmail or bribe them into being dishonest and turning on the bureau.

Ness's recruits, all in their twenties, were highly trained in areas ranging from wiretapping to truck driving to marksmanship—skills that were needed to fight an underworld figure as dangerous as Al Capone. Ness and his small, loyal force of officers were dubbed "The Untouchables" by the underworld because they could neither be bought off nor frightened away.

Raised in New York City, Al Capone had dropped out of school in the sixth grade after beating up one of his teachers. From then on, he learned his lessons on the street, especially as a member of the James Street Gang.

Because he knew government agents could sometimes be bribed into helping the underworld, Eliot Ness (1902-1957) selected only the most honest men for his "Untouchables" unit.

An older criminal named James Torrio ran this group of young boys as a subsidiary of the notorious Five Points Gang, which Capone eventually joined. One of Capone's closest friends, both in school and in the gang, was Charles "Lucky" Luciano, who would also become a major crime boss. The two men remained lifelong friends.

When Capone was in his late teens, Torrio hired him as a bouncer in a saloon-brothel the older gangster ran in Brooklyn. While working there, Capone picked up a huge knife scar on his left cheek in a fight with a tough hood named Frank Galluccio. In 1920, Torrio relocated to Chicago to help out his uncle, Big Jim Colosimo, one of the city's leading mobsters. Torrio summoned Capone from Brooklyn to assist him. That year, Luciano also moved to Chicago.

Torrio wanted to take advantage of Prohibition and gain control of the liquor racket, an undertaking that promised profits by the millions. But Colosimo, who was already rich and content, said he saw no need to expand and kept Torrio from moving ahead with this plan. Torrio decided to "eliminate" Colosimo and then take over Big Jim's organization. Torrio and Capone plotted Colosimo's murder and hired Brooklyn-based killer Frankie Yale to do the job.

Now the Torrio-Capone combination was on the move. The two hoodlums took over some gangs that bowed to their threats and went to war with others that failed to cooperate. Their biggest hit was the 1924 assassination of Dion O'Banion, the head of the North Side Gang. To accomplish this, the two gang leaders once again used the talents of Frankie Yale.

The O'Banion killing, however, soon resulted in all-out war with the rest of the North Siders. Torrio was badly shot in an ambush and hovered near death in a hospital for days. When he left the hospital, he told Capone, "Al, it's all yours." Torrio then retired and moved back to Brooklyn with an estimated $30 million.

By early 1925, Capone now found that he needed to use brains as well as muscle to run his criminal operations. He had become a top executive, heading a firm employing more than 1,000 people with a weekly payroll of $300,000. Capone's secret to success was to limit his mob's activities mainly to rackets that enjoyed strong demand from the public: liquor, gambling, and prostitution. His motto was: "Give the people what they want, and you have to gain a measure of popularity."

Like Eliot Ness, Al Capone surrounded himself with men he could trust. To prove his generosity, Capone hired Galluccio—the thug who had scarred him—as a bodyguard. Still, Capone faced many assassination attempts, including one effort to poison his soup.

In September 1926, the O'Banion gang sent an entire convoy of cars loaded with machine-gunners past Capone's hotel headquarters in Cicero, Illinois. The gunmen poured in 1,000 rounds, but Capone escaped injury.

One by one, Capone eliminated his North Side enemies and others who resisted his will. Capone also had disloyal members of his own organization killed.

By now, Capone seemed impossible to stop. In 1927, his organization grossed $60 million of the $105 million that the the Chicago underworld took in that year. Capone, however, erred terribly when he ordered the "St. Valentine's Day Massacre" to kill Bugs Moran, the only important member in the O'Banion gang who was still alive. Masquerading as police officers, Capone's hit men machine-gunned to death Moran and six other men on St. Valentine's Day in 1929. Suddenly, the public had enough of the savage Prohibition wars. With the help of Eliot Ness, officials in Washington, D.C., began applying intense pressure to end organized crime.

Ness, who took delight in personal publicity, informed the press whenever he planned a major raid on a brewery. Although the photographers who descended on the scene of the raid often got in Ness's way, his superiors did not interfere because the resulting news coverage showed ordinary citizens—as well as members of the underworld—that Capone was not invulnerable. The Untouchables also distracted Capone while other agents infiltrated his organization to gain evidence for the tax-evasion charges that would one day lead to his conviction.

After helping to put Capone behind bars, Ness became the Justice Department's chief investigator of

In 1931, Al Capone (1899-1947) was sentenced to prison for income tax evasion even though the public knew he was guilty of far worse crimes than not paying his taxes.

Prohibition violations in Chicago. He was later assigned to the "moonshine mountains" of Tennessee, Kentucky, and Ohio. In 1935, a reform administration in Cleveland, Ohio, installed Ness as its new public safety director. At that time, a vicious gang known as the Mayfield Road Mob controlled Cleveland's gambling, bootlegging, and prostitution operations, which had spread to virtually every neighborhood in the city. Labor racketeers were strangling the building trades, and violence was ever present. Gang killings were almost as prevalent as they had been in Chicago during its worst period.

Ness quickly established a new environment in the city and rooted out corruption in the police department. He ordered mass transfers and fired officers for such offenses as taking bribes or being drunk on duty. Ness also established the Cleveland Police Academy.

During his six-year tenure as director of public safety, Ness was the object of shootings, beatings, threats, and an attempted police frame-up. But in the end, his efforts crushed the Mayfield Road Mob and forced syndicate bosses to move their gambling operations outside the city limits.

Ness left his Cleveland post during World War II to become federal director of the Division of Social Protection for the Office of Defense. In this capacity, he directed programs to combat venereal disease at every military base in the United States. For this work, Ness received the navy's Meritorious Service Citation in 1946.

Only after World War II did Ness finally use his college training in economics and enter the business world. With his wife, Betty, and son, Bobby, he moved to Coudersport, Pennsylvania. There, he became president of the Guaranty Paper and Fidelity Check Corporation.

Ness also spent more than two years working on *The Untouchables*, a book about his career in the FBI. But Eliot Ness did not live to see the finished product. On

May 16, 1957, shortly after approving the book's final proofs, he died suddenly of a heart attack.

As one of the most famous law officers in American history, Eliot Ness and his agents caused the Capone organization grievous financial harm and serious inconvenience. But claims made by the law officer and his biographers sometimes bordered on fiction. He did not immediately defeat Capone's underworld empire. Nor did the Untouchables completely dry up all bootlegging activity in the city of Chicago. Despite their efforts, the city was never completely free from organized crime. Still, Ness did justify his reputation as the head of an incorruptible unit of officers in an era when honest law enforcers were not easy to find.

*Although Senator Estes Kefauver (1903-1963)
made many political enemies, he won the trust of
the American people.*

6

Estes Kefauver
A Crusader in Congress

*A*lways dedicated to helping "the little people," Tennessee senator Estes Kefauver tackled some of the toughest institutions in the United States during his time in office. Using his power as an elected official, Kefauver launched investigations into big-business monopolies and underworld crime. But he alienated some of his political allies while trying to end corruption in government.

Carey Estes Kefauver was born on July 26, 1903, in Madisonville, Tennessee, to Phredonia Estes and Robert Kefauver. In the summer of 1916, when he was 13, Estes (as he liked to be called) helped his father to distribute campaign posters for President Woodrow Wilson. The following year, his mother took him to Washington, D.C., where he met her cousin Joseph Folk, a former governor of Missouri. Impressed by his visit to the U.S. capital, Estes proclaimed that he wanted to become a lawyer and eventually enter politics.

Intent on his dream, Estes Kefauver attended law school at Yale University after graduating from the University of Tennessee. In 1927, when he was 24, he graduated from Yale with honors. In his first year of practice, Kefauver earned only $800 and learned much about the poor. He accepted many black clients at a time when public facilities in the South were segregated and many white people believed that blacks were inferior. But Kefauver thought all people, regardless of their race, deserved equal protection under the law.

In 1934, Kefauver fell in love with a dress designer from Scotland named Nancy Pigott. The two were married the following year. At this time, Kefauver was a member of the Volunteers, a local group dedicated to stopping corruption in government. While he practiced law, the newly married attorney also wrote a series of articles in the *Chattanooga News* concerning public power and local government reform. These articles gained him public attention.

Aware of corruption in local politics, Kefauver began to believe he might be able to do more to attack the problem by holding office himself. In 1939, when the congressman who had served Tennessee's third district for 16 years died, Kefauver decided that the time had come to enter politics on the Democratic ticket. The *Chattanooga Times* supported Kefauver's candidacy but said: "It is something of a paradox that Mr. Kefauver, who is perhaps best known in this county as an enemy of machine politics, is the avowed candidate of most machines throughout the district."

In the special election, Kefauver defeated his Republican opponent by a 3-to-1 margin and was off to Washington, D.C. Kefauver was 36 years old and eager to move up in the political world, confident that this was only the beginning.

Kefauver quickly made an impression on his fellow legislators. Though he was quiet and mannerly, Kefauver did not hesitate to speak his mind about issues such as congressional reform and the rights of legitimate businesses. Because of Kefauver's hard work, Tennessee's third district elected to keep him in Congress in the 1940 election. Now he could continue to fight for the causes he cared about most—especially the public utility called the Tennessee Valley Authority (TVA). Created by Congress in 1933, the TVA was an independent corporate agency designed by the U.S. government to meet the energy needs of Tennessee and the surrounding areas.

Despite its success, the TVA was under attack from the private power companies, which considered it unfair competition. By subsidizing the *Chattanooga Free Press*, one power company had managed to eliminate the TVA's champion, the competing *Chattanooga News*, for which Kefauver had written. Even worse, Kenneth McKellar, the Democratic senator from Tennessee, introduced legislation in Congress that would have returned control of the TVA to politicians and the private power companies.

But McKellar had not reckoned on Kefauver, who addressed the House of Representatives in May 1942 and

Established by an act of Congress in 1933, the Tennessee Valley Authority was different from most federal agencies because its officials did not work out of Washington, D.C., but instead were headquartered in Tennessee.

Like Estes Kefauver, Tennessee senator Kenneth McKellar (left) saw corruption in government, but the two men defined "corruption" in different ways.

led off the fight for the TVA with an impressive defense of the agency. "Not a dollar has been embezzled or misspent," Kefauver said. His speech sent McKellar's proposal down to defeat. In November 1944, Kefauver was once again returned to Washington, D.C., with a 3-to-1 victory margin.

By 1948, Kefauver felt the time had come for him to enter the U.S. Senate. During his campaign, the Republican press—as well as Tennessee Democratic congressman and "political boss" Edward Crump—attacked Kefauver for being "Communistic." Some political observers complained that Crump, who had boulevards, a stadium, and a bridge named after him, *was* Tennessee government.

Then something happened that would change Kefauver's political fortunes. On June 10, 1948, an advertisement appeared in every daily newspaper in Tennessee. The headline read, "Estes Kefauver Assumes the Role of Pet Coon." (The word *coon* is another name for raccoon.) The rest of the ad said:

> Kefauver reminds me of the pet coon that puts its foot in an open drawer of your room, but invariably turns its head while its foot is feeling around in the drawer. The coon hopes, through its cunning by turning its head, he will deceive any onlookers as to where his foot is and what it is into.

The text was boldly signed by E. H. Crump, who favored Kefauver's political opponent, incumbent senator Tom Steward. Estes Kefauver chose to fight back in a simple but dramatic way. Before a large crowd that had gathered to hear him in the Peabody Hotel in Memphis, Tennessee, he stood and began to speak about raccoons. "The coon is a clean animal," Kefauver declared. "It washes its food before eating. The coon is an American animal; it is found nowhere else in the world. The coon is a courageous animal; it can lick its weight in dogs any day." He then said defiantly, "I may be a coon, but I'm not Mr. Crump's pet coon."

In the middle of his talk, Kefauver reached down into the paper bag at his side, pulled out a coonskin cap, and placed it on his head. The result was electrifying. Now, whenever he spoke in public, Kefauver wore the coonskin cap. And wherever he went, applause greeted

Edward Crump (1876-1954), who served as a Tennessee congressman and mayor of Memphis, planned to get even with Estes Kefauver for challenging his longtime political influence with Tennessee voters.

him and his hat. Crump's attack had backfired so badly that it resulted not only in a Kefauver victory but also in the destruction of Crump's political hold over the state. (With the coonskin cap, many people said Kefauver resembled nineteenth-century adventurer and congressman Davy Crockett. "The Ballad of Davy Crockett," a television show based loosely on his life, was popular during the 1950s. Ironically, a distant relative on Kefauver's mother's side of the family had run against Crockett in an election.)

Kefauver believed the time was ripe to investigate the criminal underworld's ties to big business. Was there really such a thing as a crime syndicate, and did it have influence over lawmakers and law enforcers? Was there actually a movement toward a monopoly in the crime world? If so, was there anything that Congress could do to protect the public?

Getting authorization for such an investigation was not easy. Kefauver's resolution to have the Senate investigate organized crime would have to pass the Senate's Judiciary Committee. The chairman of that committee was Pat McCarran, whose home state of Nevada was largely influenced by gambler-businessmen and their criminal associates. As a member of the Judiciary Committee, Kefauver kept after the reluctant McCarran. When newspapers began asking why the investigation was being held up, the Nevada senator finally agreed to proceed with the investigation.

Kefauver's Special Committee to Investigate Crime in Interstate Commerce would become known to millions of Americans as the "Kefauver Committee." This committee had the authority to borrow both personnel and facilities from any federal agency, including the FBI and the Secret Service. In addition, Kefauver had his own staff of about ten investigators.

The Kefauver Committee received help from the Federal Communications Commission, which requested telephone companies to keep a permanent record of the details of all long-distance calls. (The telephone was the basic tool of people placing illegal bets.) From the Department of Justice and its attorneys all over the country, the committee amassed information on 150 criminals, many of whom used underworld aliases like "The Enforcer," "Jimmy Blue Eyes," and "Trigger Mike."

Members of the Kefauver Committee held hearings in several cities across the United States. When the hearings were broadcast on national television, Kefauver's name became a household word. Reading newspaper stories about faceless mobsters testifying before the committee was one thing. But it was something else to actually see these mobsters and their political cronies on the television screen, squirming as they answered tough questions.

One after another, law officers from Florida to Louisiana to New York admitted to making money by working with the underworld. Kefauver estimated that organized crime was taking in approximately $20 million annually. He issued a report saying that the Mafia—an organized crime network based in Sicily, Italy—was behind a major crime syndicate in New York and that hoodlums had infiltrated many legitimate businesses throughout the United States.

One of the most notorious men Kefauver confronted was Frank Costello, who reportedly received $10,000 from a fire fighters' union that sought to win his support. Costello, who had investments in the real estate, oil, gambling, and ice cream industries, insisted that the television cameras show only his hands on the air.

In 1950, Kefauver publicly attacked Wisconsin senator Joseph McCarthy for violating individual rights during McCarthy's investigations into Communists in government and the entertainment industry. Kefauver believed it was his duty to defend the rights of all law-abiding citizens—even those who opposed the nation's political system.

Although Kefauver had become an American hero, he was making political enemies—even within his own party. He had enraged many Democrats by showing that some members of the Democratic Party had been involved in illegal activities. Kefauver unknowingly upset Democratic president Harry Truman, who did not tolerate disloyalty within the party.

Kefauver stepped down from the chairmanship of the committee after almost one year and returned home to assess the impact of the crime investigation on the American people and on his own political future. Hearing nothing but overwhelming public support, he decided to run for the presidency in the 1952 election.

Kefauver met with President Truman, who had decided not to run for reelection, and told him about his plans to seek the presidency. After speaking with Truman, he became convinced that he had the president's support. Soon afterward, Kefauver made a formal announcement that he was going to seek the Democratic nomination for the presidency of the United States.

Kefauver, wearing his trademark coonskin cap, meets with young supporters during his 1952 presidential campaign.

Kefauver, who captured 14 victories in the 16 Democratic primaries, had good reason for optimism when he arrived at the Democratic National Convention in Chicago in 1952. Public opinion polls consistently marked Kefauver as the most popular candidate. With the largest number of pledged delegates, Kefauver felt confident that the party would name him the Democratic presidential candidate.

Harry Truman, however, finally decided that Illinois governor Adlai Stevenson—not Kefauver—should become the nation's next president. When Truman arrived at the convention, he requested that Kefauver withdraw in favor of Stevenson. Bowing to the president's wishes, Kefauver pledged that he would release his delegates so that they could vote for Stevenson.

The next day, leaders of the Democratic Party gathered to choose Stevenson's running mate. Stevenson's first choice was Kefauver, but Truman and the other politicians vetoed his choice and instead went for Senator John Sparkman of Alabama. This action outraged thousands of Kefauver's supporters across the United States, who were angered that the president and other Democratic officials had overlooked Kefauver because he had exposed crime and graft in the Truman administration. Speaker of the House Sam Rayburn used to tell every freshman class of new representatives in Congress, "To get along, go along." Estes Kefauver had ignored this advice, and now he was paying the price.

Harry Truman (1884-1972), president of the United States from 1945 to 1953, resented Estes Kefauver for publicly shaming the Democratic Party.

By this time, the powerful private utility corporations had set to work once again to undermine the TVA, which produced much of the electric power for Tennessee and the surrounding areas. Newly elected president Dwight Eisenhower, the first Republican president in 20 years, was easily persuaded that the TVA ought to be eliminated to lessen what some people saw as "creeping socialism" in the United States. (Eisenhower had defeated Stevenson in the 1952 election.)

Instead of supporting the TVA, the federal government planned to award a large contract to a privately held company. The contract would result in higher electric rates for the consumer and more money for the owners of the company. But Kefauver quickly stepped in and foiled their plans.

In 1957, Kefauver embarked on one of his finest achievements when he became chairman of the Senate Judiciary Committee's Subcommittee on Antitrust and Monopoly. Now he could proceed with the investigation of abuses the American people suffered from unfair business practices.

In its first investigation of corporate America, Kefauver's subcommittee went directly after one of the nation's largest industries—steel. Between the end of World War II in 1945 and the onset of the Kefauver inquiry in 1957, the steel industry had boosted its prices 12 times. Kefauver wanted to know why. He soon learned that the steel companies were playing a confusing game of "follow the leader." When one major steel company raised its prices, the other companies "competed" by raising their prices to the same point.

Kefauver didn't understand this strategy. Wouldn't lowering prices bring more sales? He pointed out that steel prices were not competitive and that the companies could sell more steel and make more profits by keeping their prices lower than their competitors.

U.S. Steel Chairman Roger Blough offered a strange defense for uniform prices by saying that if all steel prices were the same, customers were free to buy from any producer they chose. But if prices were different, then buyers would be compelled to purchase from the company with the lowest prices. After the hearings, consumers grew resentful of the industry's unfair price

Consumers were not convinced when U.S. Steel chairman Roger Blough explained that they were better off paying higher prices.

increases, and the steel companies restored competitive pricing.

Over the next few years, Kefauver's subcommittee held similar hearings to investigate auto companies, electrical manufacturing businesses, and even the baked goods industry. In July 1959, Kefauver announced that hearings on the drug industry would begin in December. He was ready to undertake what would become the greatest challenge of his life.

Kefauver was stunned by how little medicine cost to manufacture compared with how much the drug companies charged the public. He was not the only one who felt cheated about paying several dollars too much for a small bottle of pills. People all over the country had been waiting for someone to take up the fight against high drug prices.

On December 7, 1959, the subcommittee's hearings got under way. On the very first day, it became clear that the leaders of the drug industry were just as ruthless—and as unprepared for Kefauver's questions—as the steel and auto barons had been.

Kefauver used the facts his subcommittee had collected about drug research and the cost of production. He pointed out that a bottle of prednisolone (a drug used by arthritis victims) cost only $1.50 to make, yet sold for $17.90—a mark-up of more than 1,000 percent! The committee then produced a chart showing that the four largest companies sold prednisolone at the same price. The president of one pharmaceutical company said the competitive situation required those prices. When Kefauver asked the company president why his firm did not lower its prices to be more competitive, he replied that drug prices were high because the number of sick people was limited.

Over the next ten months, Kefauver slowly built his case. He decided to create a bill that would protect consumers—including the sick, the elderly, patients in hospitals, and the parents of young children.

Before he could complete the hearings or draw up the bill, Kefauver returned home for the 1960 summer primaries. In Tennessee, he discovered that he was running far behind his primary opponent. While Kefauver

Senator Estes Kefauver believed that public officials must first try to help their constituents, not their own careers.

was making a political speech near the end of his campaign, a local druggist came out of his store and began heckling him. The senator then flung out a long arm with forefinger pointed at the druggist and shouted, "There's one of your enemies!" The audience roared its approval. From then on, Kefauver made all of his speeches near a local drugstore. He used the same lines and gestures and received the same enthusiastic results. In the end, Kefauver rolled up a 2-to-1 victory margin.

With the elections out of the way, Kefauver pushed for a drug bill that would lower prices, increase competition, and help to protect America's health. Even though the hearings were scheduled to continue on into February 1962, Kefauver submitted his drug bill in April 1961. The bill passed the Senate, but it was not signed by President John F. Kennedy.

But a terrible tragedy kept Kefauver's bill alive. On July 15, 1962, the *Washington Post* carried a front-page story headlined "Heroine of FDA Keeps Bad Drug Off Market." A medical officer on staff at the Food and Drug Administration (FDA) had been suspicious about the side effects of thalidomide, a tranquilizer used in sleeping pills. Thalidomide had been commonly used in Europe since 1957, but it had never received approval by the FDA in the United States.

West Germany revealed that more than 7,000 babies had been born there without arms and legs, with their hands and feet attached directly to the body trunk.

Without the FDA, thalidomide would have been available in the United States and thousands more children would have been born with birth defects. The next day, U.S. newspapers published heartbreaking photographs of mal-formed infants. In light of this sensational news about the drug, President Kennedy signed Kefauver's bill into law on October 10, 1962.

Kefauver had redeemed himself as a national hero once more, but his life would come to an end ten months later. In August 1963, as Kefauver rose to make a speech on the Senate floor, he felt a severe pain in his heart. He paused, still in obvious discomfort, then finished his speech. Two days later, Estes Kefauver died of a rup-tured artery.

As one of the more powerful men in Washington, Estes Kefauver was adamant about using his power to help the people of the United States. Unlike some of his colleagues, Kefauver marked his political career with personal courage and integrity.

Over the past five decades, Holocaust survivor Simon Wiesenthal has tracked down more than 1,000 Nazi criminals.

7

Simon Wiesenthal
Nazi Hunter

*S*imon Wiesenthal is a survivor of the Holocaust, the mass murder of European Jews by the Nazis during World War II. The Allied forces of the United States, Great Britain, and the Soviet Union liberated the Nazi death camps near the end of the war and freed Wiesenthal and other Jewish prisoners. Afterward, Wiesenthal dedicated his life to documenting the crimes of the Holocaust and hunting down the Nazi war criminals still at large.

Wiesenthal's explanation for his determination has not changed over the years: He does not want future generations to look back and see that the Nazis were able to kill more than 6 million people and not be punished for their crimes.

If there is one man who has become a reminder of the Nazis' heinous crimes and a warning for the future, it is Simon Wiesenthal. He founded the Jewish Documentation Center in Linz, Austria, immediately after World War II. The center has operated independently and with the cooperation of the governments of the United States, Germany, Israel, and Austria ever since.

Wiesenthal has been personally responsible for making the public aware of many brutal Nazi criminals, including Franz Murer (known as "the Butcher of Wilno"), who was responsible for the death of approximately 80,000 Jews, and Erich Rajakowitsch, who supervised transports to the death camps from Holland. Wiesenthal has also written his memoirs, which describe the horrors of Nazi death camps and his hope that such atrocities will never happen again.

Simon Wiesenthal was born in 1908 in Buchach, a small town in the Galicia province of the Austro-Hungarian Empire. Simon and his mother were often discriminated against because they were Jewish. (Simon's father died during World War I.) One university would not accept Simon because the administrators placed rigid limits on the number of Jewish students they would accept. Because of this, Wiesenthal went to Prague, Czechoslovakia, where he earned a degree in architectural engineering from the Polytechnic University in 1932. Four years later, he married Cyla Müller and started a small architectural firm in the eastern Polish city of Lvov.

At the beginning of World War II, when the Soviet Army occupied Lvov, Soviet soldiers arrested and killed Wiesenthal's stepfather because he owned a factory. They also forced Wiesenthal to close his business and take a menial job in a bedspring factory.

In 1941, the Germans displaced the Soviets in controlling Lvov. Through the help of a sympathetic police officer, Wiesenthal narrowly escaped execution by the Nazis. However, Nazi soldiers later arrested Wiesenthal and his wife for being Jewish. At first, they kept him in the Janowska concentration camp just outside Lvov. Then, the Nazis sent the Wiesenthals, as part of a huge forced-labor unit, to a large railroad repair shop near Janowska. She polished brass fittings, and he was forced to paint German eagles and swastikas on locomotives.

In 1942, the Nazis began to order their commanders to implement the "Final Solution." Nazi leader Adolf Hitler intended to kill the Jewish people living in areas conquered by German troops, and the outside world did little to help the Jews. British authorities were reluctant to accept the evidence coming from refugees. Although

German dictator Adolf Hitler (1889-1945), who rose to power in 1933, intended to create an Aryan "master race" of people of German and Nordic descent.

many Americans sympathized with the victims of Nazi persecution, President Franklin Roosevelt wanted to avoid entering the war, which had begun in 1939 when Germany invaded Poland. In the meantime, the Nazis imprisoned millions of people in the death camps.

By September 1942, almost all of Wiesenthal's family and his wife's family were dead. Wiesenthal's mother died in a concentration camp, and his wife's mother had been shot to death by Ukrainian police on the steps of her house.

While working in the German railroad repair shop, Wiesenthal met with members of the Polish underground, who were fighting against the Nazi occupiers of Poland. He gave them detailed charts of railroad junctions that saboteurs could use to disrupt Nazi transportation. In exchange, the underground provided Wiesenthal's wife, Cyla, with false papers that identified her as a Polish woman named Irene Kowalska. With these documents, Wiesenthal's wife escaped in 1942. She lived in Warsaw for two years, and then worked as a forced laborer in Germany's Rhineland. The Nazis never discovered her true identity.

Wiesenthal escaped from the railroad camp in 1943, just a few weeks before the Nazis began murdering

Millions of Jewish people suffered in concentration camps during the murderous years of the Nazi regime, which lasted from 1933 to 1945.

In an effort to "purify" the human race, the Nazis murdered 6 million Jews, as well as thousands of Gypsies, mentally retarded people, and others.

all the inmates there. A combination of friendship, bribery, and luck enabled him to escape. But the Nazis recaptured him weeks later and sent him back to the Janowska camp, where he faced certain death. Janowska had held nearly 150,000 prisoners, and the Nazis killed all but 35 of them.

Simon Wiesenthal was among the 35 who survived. He would have died, too, if his arrival at Janowska had not coincided with the sudden collapse of the Nazi eastern front and the rapid advance of the Soviet Army. The 200 guards at Janowska forced the 35 remaining prisoners to march with them away from the advancing army and toward Mauthausen in upper Austria. Most of the 35 prisoners were half starved and exhausted from forced labor, and they died during the strenuous march. Wiesenthal survived.

On May 5, 1945, a U.S. Army armored unit liberated Mauthausen. There, the soldiers found Wiesenthal, weighing a gaunt 110 pounds, in a barracks filled with dead and dying prisoners. Simon Wiesenthal's will to survive had kept him alive. He now set out on a mission to gather evidence about Nazi atrocities for the U.S. Army. He worked with the U.S. Office of War Crimes section. When the war finally ended later that year, Wiesenthal began to work for the U.S. Army Counter-Intelligence Corps. Late in 1945, Wiesenthal and his wife, Cyla, were reunited. Their only child, Paulinka, was born in 1946.

*Simon Wiesenthal worships in a synagogue in 1946,
one year after he was liberated from the Nazis.*

By 1947, the United Nations Wartime Commission had secured detailed files on Nazi war criminals. At that time, the Allies decided to allow the International War Crimes Tribunal, which was set up in Nuremberg, Germany, to try the captured Nazis who had committed the most vicious and inhumane crimes.

At the Nuremberg Trials, Holocaust survivors provided riveting testimony on Nazi atrocities, but the world soon lost interest in the Holocaust. Many nations became more concerned with the spread of communism. Also, many former Nazis had professional skills and were valuable to both governments and businesses in the United States, Great Britain, Canada, and other nations, which sometimes overlooked the Nazis' past crimes.

Frustrated by the Allies' loss of interest in hunting down Nazis, Simon Wiesenthal opened the Jewish Documentation Center in Linz to assemble evidence for the trials that he hoped would take place. In 1954, he closed the Linz office and turned the files over to Israel for placement in the Yad Vashem archives.

Wiesenthal gave Israel everything but his dossier on Adolf Eichmann, the Nazi official in charge of implementing Hitler's extermination plan. Wiesenthal continued his investigations and was asked to administer an occupational training school for refugees from Hungary and other Eastern European nations. At night and on weekends, Wiesenthal concentrated on finding the elusive Eichmann, who had gone into hiding after the war ended.

News about former Nazis came to him from a network of friends and supporters all over Europe. Wiesenthal became a living clearance center for facts that might help to find Eichmann and other criminals who had been high-ranking Nazis. Wiesenthal also worked closely with Israeli agents. Combining their efforts, they located Eichmann in 1960 in Argentina.

Wiesenthal's success in locating Eichmann and the publicity of the Nazi's trial in Jerusalem brought new promises of support for the ongoing search for other Nazis still living in freedom. "We have just scratched the surface," Wiesenthal said. "The majority of former Nazis who committed serious crimes is still free." Encouraged by well-wishers in Israel and the United States, Wiesenthal reopened his Jewish Documentation Center—this time in Vienna—and he devoted himself exclusively to Nazi-hunting. In 1962, Eichmann was tried and hanged for his crimes against humanity.

High on Wiesenthal's list of targets was a man named Karl Silberbauer, the Nazi officer who had arrested Anne Frank. This 14-year-old Jewish girl had died in a Nazi concentration camp after hiding in a now-famous attic in Amsterdam with her family for almost two years. After the war, her father discovered her diary in the attic and had it published, but Nazi supporters in Holland discredited it. (In 1952, *The Diary of Anne Frank*

Adolf Eichmann, seated within a protective glass booth, went on trial in Jerusalem in 1962.

While hiding in an attic in Amsterdam, Anne Frank wrote in her diary that, in spite of the brutal crimes she had seen, she still believed that most people were basically good.

was first published in the United States.) Simon Wiesenthal located Silberbauer, who was serving as a police inspector in Austria. When he confronted Silberbauer, the former Nazi confessed, "I arrested Anne Frank."

By 1966, Wiesenthal had located several former Nazi officers, who were put on trial in West Germany for killing Jews in Lvov. Then, Wiesenthal began looking for Franz Stangl, commandant of the Treblinka concentration camp in Poland. More than 800,000 people had been hanged, shot, and gassed to death under Stangl's command. A network of Wiesenthal informants heard rumors that Stangl was in Argentina or Cuba, but Wiesenthal finally located him in Brazil. The pressure

Wiesenthal exerted, in addition to the worldwide publicity Stangl received, resulted in Stangl's deportation to West Germany for imprisonment in 1967.

By the end of the year, Wiesenthal came to the United States to be interviewed by the media and to address various groups about the Nazis he was hunting. The visit was also designed to shore up support for the Jewish Documentation Center in Vienna and to reinforce American members of his network. (Despite Wiesenthal's success at bringing Nazis to trial, some people still supported the hateful beliefs of Adolf Hitler. By 1967, Neo-Nazi groups were being formed in Linz and other cities.)

When he arrived in the United States, Wiesenthal boldly announced that Hermine Ryan—a married, New York homemaker—was actually a Nazi named Hermine Braunsteiner, who had supervised the murder of several hundred children during World War II. According to Wiesenthal, she and her colleagues would throw young children into the air, slash their eyes with a whip, then shoot bullets into their faces. Her husband, Russell, insisted that she was too gentle to hurt anyone, but the documentation of Braunsteiner's guilt was too strong. She was deported to West Germany in 1973 to stand trial and was sentenced to life in prison.

Simon Wiesenthal does not track down each fugitive by himself. His task is to gather and analyze evidence. He is assisted by a vast information network of Jews and non-Jews. Many of them are friends and colleagues, but

Franz Stangl, who oversaw the deaths of nearly 1 million people at the Treblinka concentration camp (below), avoided prison more than 20 years after the end of World War II until Simon Wiesenthal brought him to justice.

others are sympathizers he has never met. A few World War II veterans of the German army also volunteer information to Wiesenthal. The horrors these men witnessed during the war appalled them, and they, too, want to help track down the people responsible. Wiesenthal has said that he has occasionally received tips from former Nazis who were suffering from guilt or who held a grudge against other former Nazis.

When searching for information about a former Nazi, Wiesenthal combs every available document in detail. He reads the personal accounts of survivors and compares them until a pattern emerges, and he can put together sufficient information for action against a Nazi war criminal.

Wiesenthal has been described as having the thoroughness of a great scholar and the investigative mind of a good cop. He admits that he is happiest when he finds some obscure or apparently irrelevant piece of information and puts it together with other incomplete facts to build a case. Authorities know that when Simon Wiesenthal brings them a case, it is generally solid. Although his work has earned him prominent awards from several nations, he is honored most by the successful prosecutions that rely upon the evidence he and his international volunteer network have unearthed.

In addition to his skills as a detective, Wiesenthal is also a gifted persuader. Once he has enough evidence to prove that someone was a Nazi criminal, he must continue to convince the authorities and the public that it is in society's best interest to put that individual on trial, regardless of how old the evidence is or how difficult it was to obtain.

Today, Simon Wiesenthal continues to believe that the only proper punishment for a war criminal is one given out by the courts. He opposes vigilante assassinations or any other extreme measures, even in those cases where the known Nazis cannot be brought to trial.

Wiesenthal becomes most angry when he discovers a Nazi in a position of importance and influence in industry or, even worse, government. Often prosecution follows. The case of Kurt Waldheim, the former secretary general of the United Nations, presented unique and difficult problems for Simon Wiesenthal. In 1986, the *New York Times*, the World Jewish Congress, and other organizations exposed the Nazi past of Waldheim, who was then a presidential candidate of Austria. Waldheim insisted that the stories about him were lies. Despite the furor this scandal created, he was elected president of Austria.

Simon Wiesenthal began an investigation into Waldheim's past, and Austria—upon Wiesenthal's recommendation—appointed an international commission to study the Waldheim case. In 1987, Wiesenthal suggested that Kurt Waldheim resign from office because his political tactics were isolating Austria from other nations. Later that year, Waldheim finally admitted that he had been a member of the Nazi Party. But he said that he joined the organization merely to advance his career and had not been involved in Hitler's "Final Solution" to exterminate the Jewish people. The commission concluded, however, that Waldheim had been fully aware of the Nazi murders during the early 1940s, even if he wasn't directly involved in them.

Throughout his career, Simon Wiesenthal's motto has been: "I am fighting for the truth, the historic truth—without emotions." In the pursuit of that goal, he has been unyielding in his public criticism of countries that refuse to move aggressively against known Nazis. For

Although he later lied about his wartime activities, Kurt Waldheim was a German Army officer during World War II and knew of the brutal murders committed by the Nazis.

several years, he protested the Canadian government's failures to prosecute several hundred known Nazis living there, many of whom Wiesenthal located. He has said that he will not visit Canada until that country brings the alleged key Nazi criminals to trial.

Over the years, Wiesenthal's determination has made him a legend, and threats on Wiesenthal's life by telephone and by mail are quite frequent. (In 1983, a bomb destroyed the front door of the brick house in the middle-class Viennese suburb where he lives.) But the threat of violence has not stopped Wiesenthal from searching for former Nazis and speaking out against racial intolerance. His secret weapon has been his complete dedication to his cause.

He wrote once that "forgiveness is a personal matter. You have the right to forgive what has been done to you personally. You do not have the right to forgive what has been done to others."

Bibliography

Adler, Larry. *The Texas Rangers.* New York: David McKay Company, 1979.

Anderson, Jack, and Fred Blumenthal. *The Kefauver Story.* New York: Dial Press, 1956.

Arruda, George W. "Eliot Ness—Revisited." *The Investigator,* May 1988.

Ashman, Charles. *The Nazi Hunters.* New York: Pharos Books, 1988.

Bergreen, Laurence. *Capone: The Man and the Era.* New York: Simon and Schuster, 1994.

Denenberg, Barry. *The True Story of J. Edgar Hoover and the FBI.* New York: Scholastic Inc., 1993.

Gollomb, Joseph. *Scotland Yard.* London: Hutchinson, 1927.

Gribble, Leonard. *Great Manhunters of the Yard.* London: Roy Publishers, 1966.

Keating, Bern. *An Illustrated History of the Texas Rangers.* Chicago: Rand McNally, 1975.

Lavine, Sigmund. *Allan Pinkerton, America's First Private Eye.* New York: Dodd, Mead and Company, 1963.

Ness, Eliot. *The Untouchables: The Real Story.* New York: Pocket Books, 1957.

Neuberger, Richard L. *Royal Canadian Mounted Police.* New York: Random House, 1953.

Orrmont, Arthur. *Master Detective Allan Pinkerton.* New York: Messner, 1965.

Powers, Richard Gid. *G-Men: Hoover's FBI in American Popular Culture.* Carbondale: Southern Illinois University Press, 1983.

Purvis, Melvin. *American Agent.* Garden City: Doubleday, Doran, 1936.

Ramsay, A. A. W. *Sir Robert Peel.* London: Constable, 1928.

Stewart, Robert. *Sam Steele, Lion of the Frontier.* Toronto: Doubleday, 1979.

Swados, Harvey. *Standing Up for the People: The Life and Work of Estes Kefauver.* New York: Dutton, 1972.

Webb, Walter Prescott. *The Texas Rangers: A Century of Frontier Defense.* Boston: Houghton Mifflin, 1935.

Whitehead, Don. *The FBI Story: A Report to the People.* New York: Random House, 1956.

Wiesenthal, Simon. *Justice Not Vengeance.* New York: Grove Weidenfeld, 1989.

Woermser, Richard. *Pinkerton: America's First Private Eye.* New York: Walker, 1990.

Index

154

Nelson, Baby Face, *See* Gillis, Lester

Neo-Nazis, 145

Ness, Betty, 110

Ness, Bobby, 110

Ness, Eliot: as Cleveland public safety director, 109-110; death of, 110-111; early years of, 104; and fight against organized crime, 8, 89, 102, 108, 109, 111; as head of Untouchables,102, 104, 105, 107, 108, 111; in Prohibition Bureau, 104, 108-109; during World War II, 110

New Scotland Yard, 20

New York Evening Journal, 100

New York Times, 100, 148

Nixon, Richard, 92

North Side Gang, 107-108

Northfield, Minnesota, raid in, 40, 41

Northwest Mounted Police (NWMP): and defense against Indians, 53, 54, 58-59; founding of, 47, 49-50; members of, 49-51; posts of, 51-52, 53, 54, 58; and protection of railroad, 55-56, 57, *See also* Royal Canadian Mounted Police; and Royal Northwest Mounted Police

Northwest Territories, 56, 58, 64

Nuremberg Trials, 141

O'Banion, Dion, 107, 108

organized crime, 89, 90, 102, 106-108, 109-110, 111; investigated by Kefauver, 120-122

Palo Alto Prairie, 77

Peel, Sir Robert, 9, 10, 20; death of, 13; early years of, 11-12; and Metropolitan Police, 12-13; as prime minister, 13, 14; reform measures of, 12

Perkins, Frances, 99

Pierce, William, 17-18, 19

Pile O'Bones, Canada, 56

Philadelphia, 33, 34

Pigott, Nancy, 114

Pinkerton, Allan, 7, 26; and assassination threats against Lincoln, 33-35, 36; and pursuit of James Gang, 38-44; death of, 45; early years of, 27-28; and Pinkerton's National Detective Agency, 31-32, 37, 38-44; national criminal file of, 37-38; as special agent in Chicago, 29-30; work for railroads, 31, 32, 33

Pinkerton, Joan Carfrae, 28, 29, 31, 32, 45

Pinkerton, Robert, 44, 45

Pinkerton, William, 16, 28, 39, 40, 42, 44, 45

Pinkerton's National Detective Agency, 16, 31, 35, 43, 45; and capture of James Gang, 38-44; principles of, 31-32, 45, *See also* Pinkerton, Allan

Poland, 135, 136-137, 144

prednisolone, 128

private detectives, 7, 26, 27, 31, *See also* Pinkerton's National Detective Agency

Prohibition, 102, 103, 104, 106, 108, 109

prostitution, 55, 107, 109

"public enemies," 91, 93, 96, 97, 100

157

Purvis, Melvin, 8, 88; and pursuit of Dillinger, 88, 92, 93, 97-98; and pursuit of Pretty Boy Floyd, 98-99, death of, 101; early years of, 91-92; methods of, 89, 92, 97, 98; popularity of, 88, 92, 99-100, 102; resignation of, 101

railroads, 17, 19, 31, 32, 33, 34, 35, 37, 38, 40, 42, 43, 51, 56, 58, 68, 96, 135, 136, 137
Rajakowitsch, Erich, 134
Randlett, John, 78, 79
Rayburn, Sam, 124
Regina, Canada, 56-57
Republican Party, 115, 117, 125
Rio Grande, 77-78, 79, 80, 81, 83
Rio Grande City, Texas, 79-80
Roosevelt, Franklin, 136
Royal Canadian Mounted Police (RCMP), 64-65
Royal Northwest Mounted Police, 61
Ryan, Hermine, 145
Ryan, Russell, 145

Sage, Anna, 98
St. Valentine's Day Massacre, 108
Samuels, Archie, 40
Samuels, Reuben "Doc," 38-40
Samuels, Zerelda, 40
Scotland, 27-28, 114
Scotland Yard, 9, 11-16, 19-25
Secret Service, U.S., 37, 121
segregation, 114
Senate, U.S., 117, 120, 126-128, 130, 131
Sherlock Holmes, 20, 104
Silberbauer, Karl, 142, 144
Sioux Indians, 53, 54

Sitting Bull, 53-54
Six Years with the Texas Rangers, 82
slavery, 32
Smith, Colonel W. Osborne, 49-50
South Africa, 60-61
Soviet Union, 133, 135, 139
Sparkman, John, 124
speakeasies, 102
Special Branch (Scotland Yard), 16
Special Committee to Investigate Crime in Interstate Commerce, 121-122
Special Force of the Texas Rangers, 72, 73, 77, *See also* Texas Rangers
Stangl, Franz, 144-145, 146
steel industry, 126-127
Steele, Anne Macdonald, 47-48
Steele, Elmes, 47-48
Steele, Marie Elizabeth Harwood, 59-60
Steele, Samuel Benfield: death of, 63-64; and defense against Indians, 53, 54, 58-59; early years of, 47-48; and expedition to South Africa, 60-61; as officer in Northwest Mounted Police, 7, 46, 48, 49-50, 51, 52, 55, 56-60, 61-62, 65; and protection of railroad, 55-56, 57, 58; during World War I, 62
Steele, William, 69-71, 75, 86
Steward, Tom, 118
Stillwater prison, 42
Stevenson, Adlai, 124, 125
Stratton, Albert, 25
Stratton, Alf, 25
Subcommittee on Antitrust and Monopoly, 126-128

158

159

ABOUT THE AUTHOR

ROBERT ITALIA, a native of Chicago, now works in Minneapolis as a writer and editor. Since 1982, he has written more than 50 books for young readers, including *Great Auto Makers and Their Cars.*

Photo Credits

Photographs courtesy of the Minnesota Historical Society: pp. 6, 41, 44, 74; Federal Bureau of Investigation, pp. 8, 88, 94, 100; Library of Congress, pp. 10, 13, 14, 32, 36, 39, 43, 70, 76, 81, 92, 96, 103 (both), 109, 116, 119, 125, 129, 137, 138; Wide World Photos, Inc., p. 15; Pinkerton Security and Investigation Service, pp. 16, 26, 30, 31; The Bettmann Archive, pp. 20, 22, 105, 123; Western Canada Pictorial Index, pp. 46, 50, 52, 54, 55, 59, 65; Western History Collections, University of Oklahoma, pp. 66, 69, 82, 85, 87; *The Leavenworth Times*, p. 91; Indiana State Archives, p. 99; Tennessee State Library and Archives, pp. 112, 117; National Archives, p. 127; Simon Wiesenthal Center, Beit HaShoah Museum of Tolerance Library/Archives, Los Angeles, CA, pp. 132, 136, 140, 143, 144, 146 (both); and United Nations, p. 149.

Publisher's Note: The Oliver Press would like to thank Simon Wiesenthal for his enlightening comments and valuable contributions to this book. In gratitude, the publisher will donate five percent of the annual sales of *Courageous Crimefighters* to the Jewish Documentation Center in Vienna, where Mr. Wiesenthal continues his noble fight against racial intolerance.